ASPEN TRAVEL GUIDE

2024 Edition

Discovering Aspen: Uncover the Hidden Gems and Timeless Beauty of Aspen's Landscapes, Culinary Delights, Culture, and Rich Heritage with Insider Tips

By

Roy McKean

TABLE OF CONTENT

CHAPTER FOUR

NAVIGATING ASPEN

CHAPTER FIVE

ACCOMMODATION

CHAPTER NINE

OUTDOOR ACTIVITIES

CHAPTER TEN

ASPEN TRAVEL ITINERARIES

CHAPTER ELEVEN

PRACTICAL TIPS AND RESOURCES

CONCLUSION

DISCLAIMER

Welcome to our immersive travel guide! As you embark on this journey through the pages of Aspen travel guide, we want to set clear expectations. While we aim to transport you to captivating destinations and provide valuable insights, we do so without the aid of maps and images.

Why, you ask?

Our intention is simple: to stimulate your imagination and curiosity. By omitting maps, we encourage you to rely on your instincts, engage with locals, and discover hidden gems beyond the well-trodden paths. Instead of images, we invite you to paint vivid mental pictures through words and descriptions, allowing your mind to craft its unique interpretation of the places we explore.

In this text-centric guide, we prioritize storytelling, history, culture, and practical advice. We believe that your own perceptions and interpretations will make your travels more personal and memorable. It's an invitation to be present in the moment, to interact with your surroundings, and to embrace the serendipitous adventures that come your way.

So, as you delve into these pages, let your imagination soar, and let the words be your compass in this world of exploration and discovery.

INTRODUCTION

Welcome to Aspen

Aspen, Colorado, a name that resonates with elegance, adventure, and natural beauty. Nestled in the heart of the Rocky Mountains, this enchanting town welcomes you with open arms to a world where luxury meets the great outdoors. The moment you step into Aspen, you're greeted by a tapestry of experiences that seamlessly blend the allure of high-end living with the untamed wilderness that surrounds this mountain paradise.

Why Aspen?

A Playground for All Seasons

Aspen is not just a destination; it's an immersive experience that changes its hues with the seasons. Winter transforms this town into a snow-laden wonderland, attracting winter sports enthusiasts from across the globe. The pristine slopes of Aspen Mountain (Ajax) and the world-renowned Snowmass offer a haven for skiers and snowboarders, promising an adrenaline rush against a backdrop of majestic peaks.

As the snow melts away, Aspen undergoes a metamorphosis into a summer utopia. Hiking and biking trails beckon adventure seekers to explore the lush landscapes, with the Maroon Bells standing tall as the crown jewel of the Rockies. Each season brings a unique charm, ensuring that Aspen is not just a one-time destination but a place you'll yearn to return to, time and time again.

Cultural Riches in a Mountain Retreat

Beyond its natural splendors, Aspen boasts a rich cultural tapestry that adds depth to its allure. The town's history, rooted in silver mining, is palpable as you stroll through the streets lined with Victorian-era buildings. Yet, Aspen has evolved into a sophisticated cultural hub, attracting artists, musicians, and performers from around the world.

The Aspen Music Festival and School grace the town with the melodious strains of classical music, filling the mountain air with a symphony that resonates through the valleys. The Aspen Art Museum showcases contemporary works that challenge and inspire, while the Wheeler Opera House hosts an array of performances, from theater productions to film screenings.

Mountain Luxury and Hospitality

Luxury in Aspen isn't just about opulent resorts; it's a lifestyle woven into the fabric of the community. The town is home to some of the finest accommodations, from boutique hotels to lavish chalets, each offering a unique blend of comfort and sophistication. Whether you choose to unwind in a hot tub with panoramic mountain views or savor exquisite cuisine in a rustic-chic restaurant, Aspen caters to the discerning traveler with a taste for the finer things in life.

The hospitality in Aspen extends beyond the confines of the hotels. Locals welcome visitors with a warmth that reflects the genuine love for their mountain haven. Whether you're seeking insider tips on the best trails, the coziest cafes, or the most scenic spots, Aspen's residents are eager to share their love for their town.

Outdoor Adventures Beyond Imagination

For the adventure seeker, Aspen is a dream come true. Beyond the well-trodden paths, hidden gems await discovery. The Hunter Creek Trail offers a serene escape into nature, leading you through dense forests and along a babbling creek. If you're up for a challenge, the Ute Trail rewards hikers with panoramic views from Aspen's highest accessible point.

Mountain biking enthusiasts can test their skills at Snowmass Bike Park, where the thrill of downhill rides is matched only by the breathtaking mountain vistas. And for those who prefer a more leisurely pace, a hot air balloon ride over Aspen Valley provides a surreal experience, floating above the landscapes that captivate the senses.

A Culinary Odyssey in the Mountains

Aspen's culinary scene is a gastronomic journey that complements the town's natural wonders. From cozy chalet-style restaurants to upscale dining establishments, Aspen offers a diverse array of culinary delights. Local chefs craft menus that celebrate the region's flavors, often incorporating fresh, locally sourced ingredients.

As you explore Aspen's dining scene, you'll encounter a fusion of international influences, from mountain-inspired comfort food to innovative dishes that push the boundaries of culinary artistry. Each bite is a testament to the town's commitment to providing a complete sensory experience.

CHAPTER ONE

PLANNING YOUR ASPEN ADVENTURE

1.1 Setting Your Travel Goals

Embarking on a journey to Aspen is not just a physical exploration; it's an opportunity to fulfill personal travel goals and create lasting memories. Setting clear travel goals is the first step in crafting an itinerary that aligns with your aspirations, ensuring that your time in Aspen is not just a vacation but a transformative experience.

Aspen, nestled in the heart of the Rocky Mountains, offers a myriad of experiences, from world-class skiing and snowboarding to cultural events and outdoor adventures. To make the most of your visit, consider the following steps when setting your travel goals:

1. Define Your Purpose:

Before you dive into the details of your Aspen adventure, reflect on the purpose of your trip. Are you seeking an adrenaline-fueled escape on the slopes, or is your goal to immerse yourself in Aspen's rich cultural scene? Defining your purpose sets the tone for the entire journey.

If you're an avid skier, your goal might be to conquer Aspen's legendary slopes and experience the thrill of gliding down powdery mountainsides. On the other hand, if you're more inclined towards cultural exploration, your goal could involve attending Aspen's world-renowned events, such as the Aspen Music Festival or the Food & Wine Classic.

2. Prioritize Your Interests:

Aspen caters to a diverse range of interests, so prioritize what matters most to you. Whether it's outdoor adventures, artistic endeavors, or simply relaxation amidst stunning natural landscapes, understanding your priorities helps shape your itinerary.

If you're an art enthusiast, your goal might be to explore Aspen's vibrant art scene, visiting galleries and attending cultural events. For nature lovers, setting a goal to explore the picturesque Maroon Bells or embark on a scenic hike along Hunter Creek Trail ensures you connect with Aspen's natural beauty.

3. Consider Seasonal Variations:

Aspen's charm evolves with the seasons, so consider the time of year that aligns with your travel goals. The winter months offer a snowy wonderland for skiing and snowboarding enthusiasts, while the summer months provide opportunities for hiking, biking, and enjoying outdoor festivals.

Your goal might be to experience Aspen in its winter splendor, with snow-covered landscapes and the exhilarating atmosphere of winter sports. Alternatively, if you prefer milder weather and vibrant greenery, setting a goal to visit during the summer allows for a different yet equally enchanting experience.

4. Align with Personal Growth:

Travel is not just about exploring new places; it's an avenue for personal growth and self-discovery. Consider setting goals that align with your desire for growth, whether it's trying new activities, meeting new people, or stepping out of your comfort zone.

Your goal might involve learning a new skill, such as skiing or attending a photography workshop to capture Aspen's beauty. Setting intentions for personal growth ensures that your travel experience goes beyond the surface, leaving you with valuable insights and newfound perspectives.

1.2 Choosing the Best Time to Visit

Choosing the best time to visit Aspen is not just a matter of preference; it's about aligning your interests with the unique experiences each season has to offer.

Winter Wonderland: December to February

For many, Aspen is synonymous with winter wonderland, and rightfully so. The months from December to February transform this mountain town into a snowy paradise, attracting avid skiers and snowboarders from around the globe. The world-renowned Aspen Snowmass ski resorts come alive with pristine powder, offering a plethora of slopes catering to all skill levels.

The iconic Maroon Bells, surrounded by a blanket of snow, provide a breathtaking backdrop for winter enthusiasts. The town itself exudes a festive atmosphere, with charming holiday lights, cozy fireplaces, and a myriad of winter events. If your idea of a perfect vacation involves gliding down powdery slopes, experiencing the thrill of winter sports, and enjoying après-ski coziness, then the winter months are ideal for your visit to Aspen.

Spring Awakening: March to May

As the snow begins to melt and nature awakens, Aspen undergoes a magical transformation during the spring months. March to May brings milder temperatures, and the landscape starts to burst with vibrant colors. It's a season of renewal, marked by blooming wildflowers and the gradual emergence of greenery.

Spring in Aspen offers a unique blend of winter and summer activities. Skiing is still possible in the early months, especially at higher elevations, while hiking and biking trails become more accessible as the snow recedes. The transition from winter to spring also introduces a sense of tranquility, making it an excellent time for those seeking a more laid-back experience amidst the serenity of nature.

Summer Splendor: June to August

For outdoor enthusiasts and those drawn to the lively cultural scene, the summer months in Aspen are unparalleled. From June to August, the snow-capped peaks give way to a landscape adorned with blooming wildflowers, and the warm weather opens up a myriad of recreational opportunities.

Hiking and mountain biking trails beckon adventure seekers, while the Roaring Fork River becomes a playground for water activities such as rafting and fly fishing. The summer season also hosts some of Aspen's most celebrated events, including the Aspen Music Festival and the Food & Wine

Classic. If you envision a summer filled with outdoor adventures, cultural experiences, and lively festivals, plan your visit during these warm and inviting months.

Golden Autumn: September to November

As summer bids farewell, Aspen transforms into a golden-hued landscape during the fall months. From September to November, the quaking aspen trees paint the mountainsides with brilliant shades of yellow and gold, creating a stunning tapestry of colors.

Autumn in Aspen is a photographer's delight, with the changing foliage providing a scenic backdrop for exploration. The weather remains crisp and refreshing, making it an excellent time for hiking and scenic drives. Fall is also a quieter season, offering a more intimate and reflective experience for those seeking a respite from the busyness of life.

1.3 Visa and Entry Requirements

When planning a trip to Aspen, the breathtaking destination renowned for its scenic landscapes and diverse recreational offerings, it's crucial for tourists to be well-versed in the visa and entry requirements. Navigating the bureaucratic landscape can seem daunting, but a clear understanding of these essential details ensures a smooth and hassle-free entry into the enchanting world of Aspen.

Understanding U.S. Entry Requirements:

Aspen is located in the state of Colorado, within the United States. Therefore, understanding the general U.S. entry requirements is the first step for any international traveler.

While U.S. citizens do not require a visa for domestic travel, international visitors must comply with specific regulations to gain entry into the country.

Visa Requirements for International Visitors:

The United States operates a visa system that varies based on the purpose and duration of the visit. Tourists planning a trip to Aspen for leisure generally fall under the category of a B-2 tourist visa. The B-2 visa is intended for individuals visiting the U.S. for pleasure, tourism, or medical treatment.

To obtain a B-2 tourist visa, international travelers typically need to follow these steps:

1. Complete the Online Visa Application:

Start by completing the DS-160 online visa application form. This comprehensive form gathers essential information about the traveler, including personal details, travel plans, and the purpose of the visit.

2. Pay the Visa Application Fee:

Once the DS-160 is submitted, applicants are required to pay the non-refundable visa application fee. The fee varies based on the country of origin and is typically paid online through the U.S. government's designated payment system.

3. Schedule a Visa Interview:

After paying the application fee, applicants must schedule a visa interview at the U.S. embassy or consulate in their home country. The interview is a critical step in the process and provides an opportunity for consular officers to assess the applicant's eligibility for the B-2 visa.

4. Gather Supporting Documents:

Prepare a comprehensive set of supporting documents, including proof of financial ability to cover the trip, a detailed itinerary, accommodation arrangements, and evidence of strong ties to the home country to demonstrate the intent to return.

5. Attend the Visa Interview:

On the scheduled date, attend the visa interview with all required documents. The consular officer will ask questions about the purpose of the visit, travel plans, and ties to the home country. A successful interview results in the issuance of the B-2 tourist visa.

It's crucial to note that visa application processes and requirements may vary based on the applicant's country of origin. Therefore, checking with the U.S. embassy or consulate in the specific country is essential to ensure accurate and up-to-date information.

Visa Waiver Program (VWP) for Eligible Countries:

Some international travelers may be eligible to participate in the Visa Waiver Program (VWP), which allows entry into the U.S. for up to 90 days without obtaining a visa. However, travelers must be citizens of countries that are part of the VWP and must obtain approval through the Electronic System for Travel Authorization (ESTA) before boarding their flights.

To utilize the VWP:

1. Check Eligibility:

Confirm whether your country of citizenship is part of the Visa Waiver Program. The U.S. Department of State provides a list of eligible countries.

2. Apply for ESTA:

Complete the online ESTA application, providing personal information, travel details, and passport information. Approval is usually granted quickly, but it's advisable to apply at least 72 hours before departure.

3. Receive Authorization:

Once approved, travelers receive an ESTA authorization, which is valid for multiple entries within a two-year period or until the passport expires, whichever comes first.

4. Travel to the U.S.:

With a valid ESTA authorization, eligible travelers can board their flights and enter the U.S. for a stay of up to 90 days.

It's essential to note that the VWP is not suitable for all types of visits. Travelers planning longer stays or specific activities, such as work or study, should apply for the appropriate visa category.

Essential Documents for Entry into Aspen:

Regardless of the type of visa or entry method, there are certain documents that all tourists should carry to ensure a smooth entry into Aspen:

1. Passport:

A valid passport is a fundamental requirement for international travel. Ensure that your passport is valid for at least six months beyond your intended departure date.

2. Visa or ESTA Authorization:

Carry a printed copy of your visa approval notice or the ESTA authorization. Customs and Border Protection officers may request to see this document upon arrival.

3. Travel Itinerary:

Have a detailed itinerary outlining your travel plans, including accommodation reservations, activities, and departure details. This document can assist in demonstrating the purpose of your visit.

4. Proof of Financial Ability:

Carry evidence of your financial ability to cover the costs of your stay, including accommodation, meals, and activities. This could include bank statements, credit card statements, or a letter of financial support.

5. Return Ticket:

To demonstrate your intent to return to your home country, carry a copy of your return ticket or proof of onward travel.

Tips for a Smooth Entry:

1. Be Prepared:

Familiarize yourself with the specific entry requirements for your country of origin and ensure that you have all the necessary documents.

2. Arrive Early:

Arriving at the airport well in advance of your departure time allows for any unforeseen delays and ensures a stress-free boarding process.

3. Be Honest During Interviews:

Whether applying for a visa or participating in the VWP, honesty is crucial during interviews and interactions with immigration officials. Providing accurate information enhances your credibility.

4. Keep Important Documents Secure:

Safeguard your passport, visa, and other important documents. Consider making photocopies or digital copies in case of loss or theft.

5. Stay Informed About Travel Alerts:

Check for any travel alerts or updates related to your destination. Staying informed about potential changes or challenges can help you plan accordingly.

1.4 Budgeting and Money Matters

1. Determine Your Overall Budget:

Before embarking on your Aspen adventure, establish a clear budget that encompasses all aspects of your trip. Consider accommodation, transportation, meals, activities, and any additional expenses you may encounter. Having a comprehensive budget provides a realistic framework for your spending.

2. Accommodation Choices:

While Aspen offers luxurious resorts, there are also budget-friendly accommodation options available. Consider staying slightly outside the downtown area for more economical choices. Look for guesthouses, motels, or vacation rentals that cater to varying budgets while providing comfortable amenities.

3. Transportation Planning:

Decide on the mode of transportation that aligns with your budget. Aspen has a well-connected public transportation system, which can be a cost-effective alternative to renting a car. Additionally, explore shuttle services from nearby airports to Aspen, comparing prices to find the most economical option.

4. Dining Smart:

Aspen boasts a diverse culinary scene, and while there are high-end restaurants, there are also affordable dining options. Explore local markets, cafes, and smaller eateries to experience Aspen's flavors without straining your budget. Keep an eye out for happy hour specials and daily discounts.

5. Outdoor Adventures on a Budget:

Aspen is a playground for outdoor enthusiasts, and enjoying the mountains need not be an expensive endeavor. Consider purchasing lift tickets in advance or opting for multi-day passes to save on skiing or snowboarding costs. During the summer, explore hiking and biking trails for low-cost outdoor activities.

6. Explore Free and Low-Cost Attractions:

Aspen offers a plethora of free and low-cost attractions. Wander through the charming downtown area, explore art galleries, and attend community events without spending a fortune. Check the local calendar for festivals or concerts that may align with your visit.

7. Budget-Friendly Transportation within Aspen:

Aspen's compact size makes it easy to explore on foot or with affordable transportation options. Utilize the local bus system or consider renting a bike to navigate the city and surrounding areas without the expense of a car rental.

8. Consider Off-Peak Seasons:

Traveling during off-peak seasons can lead to significant savings. Accommodation prices and activity costs may be lower, allowing you to experience Aspen's beauty without the peak-season price tags.

9. Take Advantage of Discounts and Packages:

Look for discounts on activities, tours, and attractions. Many businesses in Aspen offer package deals that can provide substantial savings when bundled together. Research online or inquire locally for special promotions.

10. Be Mindful of Tipping Customs:

While it's customary to tip for services in the United States, understanding tipping norms helps manage your budget. Research appropriate tipping percentages for different services to avoid overspending on gratuities.

1.5 Essential Packing Tips

To ensure you have everything you need for an enjoyable stay, follow these essential packing tips.

1. Dress in Layers:

Aspen's mountainous terrain can bring unpredictable weather, especially if you plan on exploring outdoor activities. Packing layers allows you to adjust to temperature changes throughout the day. Bring thermal undergarments, moisture-wicking shirts, and a waterproof jacket. Even in the summer, evenings can be cool, so having a few layers on hand is always a smart choice.

2. Comfortable Footwear:

Whether you're strolling through the town, hiking mountain trails, or navigating snowy slopes, comfortable footwear is a must. Pack sturdy walking shoes for exploring, and if visiting during the winter, consider waterproof boots to keep your feet warm and dry in the snow.

3. Sun Protection:

Aspen boasts plenty of sunny days, so sun protection is vital. Pack high SPF sunscreen, sunglasses with UV protection, and a wide-brimmed hat. The mountain altitude intensifies the sun's effects, making these items essential for a comfortable and safe outdoor experience.

4. Hydration Essentials:

The high altitude and dry climate can lead to dehydration, so bring a reusable water bottle to stay hydrated throughout your adventures. If you plan on hiking or engaging in strenuous activities, consider electrolyte supplements to replenish minerals lost at higher altitudes.

5. Camera and Binoculars:

Aspen's landscapes are nothing short of breathtaking, so don't forget your camera or smartphone for capturing the stunning views. Binoculars can also enhance your experience, especially if you're keen on birdwatching or simply want a closer look at the surrounding mountains.

6. Daypack for Outdoor Excursions:

For day trips and outdoor adventures, a reliable daypack is invaluable. Choose one with enough room for essentials like snacks, a water bottle, a map, and an extra layer. Look for a pack that distributes weight evenly for added comfort during longer hikes.

7. Charging Essentials:

Aspen offers a mix of outdoor and urban experiences, so ensure your electronic devices are always ready for use. Pack chargers for your phone, camera, and any other gadgets you bring along. A portable power bank can be a lifesaver, especially if you're spending extended periods exploring without access to power outlets.

8. Travel-Friendly Toiletries:

Keep your toiletries compact and travel-friendly. Aspen's elevation may affect your skin, so include moisturizer and lip balm to combat dryness. Travel-sized shampoo, conditioner, and other personal care items help save space in your luggage.

9. Winter Accessories (If Applicable):

If visiting Aspen in the winter, pack essential winter accessories. This includes thermal gloves, a warm hat, and a scarf. Even if you don't plan on hitting the slopes, these items will keep you cozy during chilly days and nights.

10. Adaptable Wardrobe:

Aspen's blend of outdoor activities and upscale dining means you may find yourself transitioning from hiking trails to fine dining. Pack adaptable clothing that can seamlessly take you from day to night. A pair of versatile pants and a stylish but functional jacket can go a long way.

1.5.1 Travel-Friendly Luggage Options

1. Durable Hardshell Suitcases:

Description: Aspen's landscape may include rugged terrains, and having a durable hardshell suitcase can provide the necessary protection for your belongings. Look for suitcases made from materials like polycarbonate for a balance of durability and lightweight convenience.

2. Backpacks:

Description: If you plan on engaging in outdoor activities like hiking or exploring the scenic trails around Aspen, a versatile backpack is a must. Choose a backpack with multiple compartments for organized packing and consider features like padded shoulder straps for added comfort.

3. Expandable Spinner Luggage:

Description: Aspen's changing weather may require you to pack a variety of clothing, from layers for cooler temperatures to lighter options for sunny days. An expandable spinner suitcase allows you to adjust the luggage capacity based on your needs while providing easy maneuverability.

4. Convertible Duffel Bags:

Description: For those who prefer flexibility in their luggage, a convertible duffel bag is an excellent choice. These bags can be carried as traditional duffels or worn as backpacks, offering versatility for different travel scenarios.

5. Water-Resistant Travel Backpacks:

Description: Aspen's weather can be unpredictable, and a water-resistant travel backpack adds an extra layer of protection for your belongings. This is especially important if you plan on carrying electronic devices or other sensitive items.

6. Compact Carry-Ons:

Description: If you aim to streamline your travel and avoid checked baggage fees, a compact carry-on suitcase is a practical choice. Ensure it meets airline size restrictions and is equipped with features like a built-in USB charger for added convenience.

7. Rolling Duffel Bags:

Description: For those who prefer the flexibility of a duffel bag but appreciate the convenience of wheels, a rolling duffel is an ideal compromise. It combines the best of both worlds, offering ease of transportation and ample packing space.

8. Tech-Integrated Smart Luggage:

Description: Embrace the advancements in travel gear by opting for smart luggage. Some options come equipped with features like GPS tracking, built-in scales, and USB ports for charging devices, adding a tech-savvy touch to your travel experience.

CHAPTER TWO

GETTING ACQUAINTED WITH ASPEN

2.1 Overview of Aspen's Geography and Climate

Nestled within the heart of the Colorado Rockies, Aspen boasts a geographical setting that is as captivating as it is unique. Situated at an elevation of approximately 8,000 feet, the town is embraced by the Elk Mountains, contributing to its stunning panoramic views and alpine charm. The region's geographical makeup, characterized by snow-capped peaks, lush valleys, and crystal-clear rivers, forms the backdrop for a plethora of outdoor activities and recreational pursuits.

The allure of Aspen's geography lies not only in its visual splendor but also in the diverse range of experiences it offers to visitors. The Elk Mountains, standing tall and majestic, create an idyllic setting for outdoor enthusiasts. Whether it's the thrill of skiing down powdery slopes in winter or hiking along scenic trails during the summer, Aspen's geography serves as a natural playground for adventure seekers.

In winter, the landscape transforms into a serene winter wonderland, blanketed in pristine snow. Aspen becomes a haven for skiing and snowboarding enthusiasts from around the globe, drawn to its world-class slopes and challenging terrains. The crisp mountain air, combined with the pristine white landscape, creates a magical atmosphere that captivates the senses. The town itself, adorned with twinkling lights and cozy chalets, exudes a warmth that complements the winter ambiance.

As the seasons shift to summer, Aspen's geography takes on a different charm. The snow-capped peaks give way to vibrant greenery, and the valleys come alive with a riot of wildflowers. The cool mountain breeze, coupled with sunny days, creates an ideal climate for outdoor exploration. Hiking trails beckon adventurers to discover hidden gems, and mountain biking enthusiasts can navigate challenging paths with breathtaking views at every turn.

Understanding Aspen's climate is paramount for visitors seeking to make the most of their experience. Winters, with their abundance of snowfall, beckon individuals to embrace the thrill of winter sports. As temperatures often dip below freezing, it is advisable for visitors to come well-prepared with layered clothing, insulated outerwear, and accessories such as gloves and hats to ensure a comfortable experience on the slopes.

In contrast, summers in Aspen offer a welcome respite from scorching temperatures. Daytime temperatures typically range from the mid-60s to the low 80s Fahrenheit, providing an ideal climate for a myriad of outdoor activities. Hikers can explore the trails without the constraints of heavy snow, and cyclists can traverse the picturesque landscapes with ease. It's a season where the crisp mountain air invigorates the spirit, inviting visitors to savor the natural beauty that surrounds Aspen.

Regardless of the season, packing essentials is a key consideration for those venturing into Aspen's great outdoors. Sunscreen becomes a vital companion to shield against the high-altitude sun, and staying hydrated is crucial, especially during physical activities. Sturdy footwear is a must, ensuring comfort and stability on the varied terrains.

2.2 Historical and Cultural Background

Aspen's rich history is a captivating narrative that unfolds against the backdrop of the late 19th-century mining boom. Originally established as a silver mining camp in the 1870s, the town quickly evolved into a bustling hub for prospectors lured by the promise of fortune in the rugged mountains of Colorado. The streets that now echo with the sounds of modern life were once trodden by silver barons, miners, and pioneers, each contributing to the vibrant tapestry of Aspen's past.

The boom, however, was met with the inevitable bust in the form of the silver crash of 1893. This economic downturn brought considerable hardship to Aspen, as the once-thriving mining community faced challenges that echoed throughout the region. Despite the adversity, Aspen demonstrated a remarkable resilience that would shape its future.

In the mid-20th century, Aspen underwent a transformative rebirth. It emerged from the shadows of its mining history to embrace a new identity as a premier ski resort destination. The pristine mountain landscapes that once hid veins of silver now beckon winter enthusiasts from around the world. This strategic pivot not only revitalized the town's economy but also laid the foundation for the sophisticated destination that Aspen has become today.

The historic charm of Aspen is vividly preserved in its well-maintained Victorian architecture. Strolling through the streets, visitors are transported to an era where the clinking of mining tools echoed through the mountain air. The Wheeler Opera House, a grand structure erected in 1889, stands as a testament to Aspen's commitment to preserving its cultural heritage. This historic venue, with its ornate interior and classic architecture, has transformed over the years to become a cultural epicenter. Today, it hosts a diverse array of performances, from theatrical productions to musical concerts, enriching Aspen's cultural scene and providing a modern stage within an ancient backdrop.

Culturally, Aspen is a melting pot that draws residents and visitors from diverse backgrounds. Its reputation as a cultural haven is reinforced by events such as the Aspen Music Festival and School. This annual celebration of classical music attracts world-class musicians and enthusiastic audiences alike, fostering an environment where the love for artistic expression thrives. The town's commitment to the arts is further exemplified by the Aspen Art Museum, a contemporary space that showcases thought-provoking exhibits reflecting the town's progressive spirit.

Exploring Aspen's historical and cultural facets is not just a walk through the past but a journey that enhances the overall visitor experience. Museums and guided tours offer in-depth insights into the stories and characters that have shaped Aspen into the vibrant town it is today. Visitors can immerse themselves in the tales of resilience, prosperity, and cultural diversity that define Aspen's narrative, creating a deeper connection with the town and its people. These historical and cultural explorations add layers of meaning to the breathtaking landscapes and outdoor adventures that await in this mountain paradise.

2.3 Languages and Communication

English serves as the primary language of communication in Aspen, reflecting the broader linguistic landscape of the United States. However, due to its international appeal and diverse visitor demographics, it's not uncommon to hear a variety of languages spoken throughout the town.

Aspen's hospitality industry is well-equipped to cater to a global audience, with many establishments having multilingual staff capable of conversing in languages such as Spanish, German, and French. This linguistic diversity enhances the overall experience for visitors, ensuring that language barriers are minimized, and communication flows seamlessly.

For travelers seeking a more immersive experience, engaging with locals and fellow visitors often provides opportunities to discover different languages and cultures. The welcoming atmosphere of Aspen encourages cultural exchange, making it a place where connections can be forged beyond linguistic boundaries.

To enhance communication during your stay, it's advisable to familiarize yourself with common travel phrases in English. While the majority of residents and service providers speak English fluently, having a basic understanding of the local language can contribute to a more enriching and enjoyable visit.

2.4 Currency Exchange Tips

Navigating currency exchange in Aspen is a straightforward process, as the United States Dollar (USD) is the official currency. Visitors will find a range of options for currency exchange services, including banks, currency exchange offices, and ATMs conveniently located throughout the town.

Banks in Aspen typically offer competitive exchange rates and can assist with larger transactions. It's advisable to check with your bank regarding any partnership agreements or fees associated with currency exchange to ensure a transparent and cost-effective process.

Currency exchange offices, often found in popular tourist areas, provide quick and efficient services. While their rates may vary slightly, they generally offer competitive rates for common currencies.

ATMs are widely available in Aspen, allowing visitors to withdraw cash in USD. It's essential to check with your home bank regarding international transaction fees and inform them of your travel plans to avoid any disruptions in accessing funds.

Credit and debit cards are widely accepted in Aspen, making it convenient for visitors to make purchases without the need for excessive cash. However, it's advisable to inform your bank of your travel dates to prevent any potential issues with card transactions.

Aspen's status as a premier destination ensures that currency exchange services are readily accessible, providing visitors with the flexibility and convenience needed for a seamless travel experience.

CHAPTER THREE

MUST VISIT DESTINATIONS

3.1 Maroon Bells: A Symphony of Nature's Majesty

No visit to Aspen is complete without a pilgrimage to the iconic Maroon Bells, a natural wonder that stands as a testament to the majestic beauty of the Colorado Rockies. As the most photographed peaks in North America, these twin fourteeners – Maroon Peak and North Maroon Peak – cast their reflection upon the pristine waters of Maroon Lake, creating a scene of unparalleled natural splendor.

1. Getting There:

To embark on this visual odyssey, a scenic drive or shuttle service takes visitors from downtown Aspen to the Maroon Bells Scenic Area, ensuring accessibility without compromising the pristine environment. The journey itself is a feast for the eyes, with winding roads leading through dense aspen groves and alpine meadows.

2. Exploring the Maroon Bells Scenic Area:

Upon arrival, visitors are greeted by the serene Maroon Lake, surrounded by lush greenery and towering peaks. The Maroon Bells Scenic Area offers various vantage points, each providing a unique perspective of this natural masterpiece. Photographers and nature enthusiasts alike will find themselves captivated by the ever-changing play of light and shadows on the rugged mountain faces.

3. Activities:

The Maroon Bells Scenic Area caters to a variety of activities, ensuring there's something for everyone. For those seeking a leisurely experience, a stroll along the shores of Maroon Lake is a tranquil way to absorb the beauty. More adventurous visitors can explore the network of hiking trails that weave through the area, offering a closer encounter with the towering peaks.

4. Hiking Trails:

The Maroon Bells area is renowned for its hiking trails, each offering a distinct experience. The Maroon Lake Scenic Trail provides an easy, family-friendly option, circling the lake and providing numerous opportunities for photos. The Crater Lake Trail leads to a higher vantage point, rewarding hikers with breathtaking views of both Maroon Lake and Crater Lake.

5. Wildlife Watching:

Nature enthusiasts will delight in the opportunity to observe the local wildlife. The Maroon Bells area is home to various species, including elk, mule deer, and a variety of birdlife. Wildlife viewing adds an extra layer of enchantment to the overall experience, making it a must for animal lovers.

6. Photography Tips:

For photographers, timing is key. Sunrise and sunset cast the Maroon Bells in a warm, golden hue, creating a magical atmosphere. The calm waters of Maroon Lake during these hours offer the perfect mirror-like reflection, enhancing the visual spectacle. Photography enthusiasts should consider early morning or late afternoon visits for optimal lighting conditions.

7. Guided Tours:

To delve deeper into the natural and historical significance of the Maroon Bells, guided tours are available. Knowledgeable guides share insights into the geology, flora, and fauna of the region, providing a more comprehensive understanding of this natural marvel.

8. Seasonal Variations:

The Maroon Bells offer a different spectacle in each season. In summer, wildflowers carpet the meadows, creating a vibrant burst of colors. Fall brings a breathtaking display of autumn foliage, with aspen trees transforming into hues of gold and red. Even in winter, when the Maroon Bells are blanketed in snow, the scene is nothing short of enchanting.

9. Environmental Stewardship:

While enjoying the beauty of the Maroon Bells, it's essential for visitors to practice responsible tourism. The area is part of the White River National Forest, and respecting Leave No Trace principles helps preserve the pristine environment for future generations. Stay on designated trails, pack out all trash, and adhere to guidelines provided by the U.S. Forest Service.

10. Visitor Center:

The Maroon Bells Visitor Center serves as a valuable resource, offering information about the area's natural and cultural history. Visitors can learn about the delicate ecosystem of the Maroon Bells, the indigenous Ute people, and the geological forces that shaped this awe-inspiring landscape.

3.2 Aspen Mountain (Ajax)

Aspen Mountain, affectionately known as Ajax by locals, stands as a majestic sentinel in the heart of the Colorado Rockies, beckoning adventure-seekers year-round. Renowned for its challenging slopes in winter and its network of scenic trails in the warmer months, Aspen Mountain is a quintessential destination for those yearning for an alpine escape.

Winter Wonderland:

As the snow blankets the slopes of Aspen Mountain, a magical transformation occurs, turning it into a winter wonderland that attracts skiers and snowboarders from around the globe. The Aspen Snowmass Ski Resort, featuring the Ajax trails, offers a pristine playground for winter sports enthusiasts of all skill levels. From perfectly groomed runs for beginners to the daring steeps that challenge even the most seasoned athletes, Aspen Mountain provides an unparalleled skiing and snowboarding experience.

The Silver Queen Gondola, a symbol of Aspen's grandeur, whisks visitors from the heart of downtown to the mountain's summit. As the gondola ascends, the panoramic views of the surrounding Elk Mountains unfold, creating a sense of anticipation for the adventures awaiting on the slopes. Once at the top, skiers and snowboarders are greeted with a vast expanse of white powder, framed by the rugged peaks of the Rockies.

For those seeking an extra dose of adrenaline, the black diamond runs on Aspen Mountain deliver a thrilling experience. The challenging terrain includes iconic trails such as Bell Mountain, where expert skiers can navigate through glades and steeps, creating memories that linger long after the snow has melted.

Summer Serenity:

When the snow retreats, Aspen Mountain undergoes a transformation into a serene summer paradise. The mountain sheds its winter coat, revealing a lush landscape adorned with wildflowers and hiking trails. The Silver Queen Gondola, which operates during the summer months as well, provides access to a network of scenic trails suitable for hikers and mountain bikers.

The Ajax Express Trail, accessible from the summit, offers hikers stunning views of the Roaring Fork Valley and beyond. The sight of vibrant alpine flora, such as columbines and lupines, contrasts beautifully with the bluebird skies. Nature enthusiasts can also explore the Richmond Ridge Trail, which meanders through an evergreen forest, offering glimpses of local wildlife and providing a peaceful escape into the heart of the Rockies.

Mountain bikers, eager to conquer the slopes in a different manner, can descend along carefully crafted trails, experiencing the thrill of navigating through Aspen's alpine terrain. The Snowmass Bike Park, an extension of the summer adventure offerings, caters to downhill bikers with trails ranging from beginner to advanced.

The Apres Adventure Experience:

No Aspen Mountain adventure is complete without indulging in the famed après-ski and après-hike culture. Ajax Tavern, located at the base of the mountain, serves as a hub for post-adventure relaxation. Whether sipping on a craft cocktail while enjoying the mountain views or savoring a gourmet meal inspired by local flavors, Ajax Tavern provides a sophisticated yet laid-back atmosphere.

As the sun dips below the peaks, the town of Aspen comes alive with a vibrant nightlife scene. Local bars and pubs offer a chance to mingle with fellow adventurers, sharing tales of the day's conquests. The Limelight Hotel, situated just steps from the base of Aspen Mountain, is a popular spot for après-ski festivities, with live music, locally brewed beers, and a welcoming ambiance.

Practical Tips for Ajax Exploration:

For those embarking on an Aspen Mountain adventure, there are a few practical tips to enhance the experience. First and foremost, check the weather conditions and trail status before heading up the mountain. Aspen's high-altitude environment can bring rapid weather changes, so being prepared is essential.

Additionally, consider taking advantage of guided tours or lessons, especially for those new to skiing or mountain biking. Knowledgeable guides not only enhance safety but also provide valuable insights into the mountain's history and ecology, enriching the overall experience.

3.3 Independence Pass

Nestled within the heart of the Rocky Mountains, Independence Pass stands as a testament to the majesty of nature and the ingenuity of human engineering. This renowned scenic drive, connecting the town of Aspen to Twin Lakes, is an absolute must for any visitor seeking a breathtaking journey through the alpine wonders of Colorado.

Introduction to Independence Pass:

Independence Pass, situated at an elevation of 12,095 feet (3,687 meters), is one of the highest paved mountain passes in the United States. The pass is a vital link between the towns of Aspen and Twin Lakes, providing not just a means of transportation but an unforgettable adventure through some of the most stunning landscapes in the Rocky Mountains.

The Drive: A Symphony of Natural Beauty:

Embarking on the drive from Aspen, travelers are immediately greeted by the scenic beauty that makes Independence Pass legendary. The journey begins as you wind your way through dense forests, with glimpses of the Roaring Fork River meandering alongside the road. The ascent is gradual, allowing for a seamless transition from the charming streets of Aspen to the grandeur of the mountainous terrain.

As you climb higher, the landscape evolves, presenting a picturesque mix of alpine meadows, wildflowers, and imposing mountain peaks. The road, skillfully engineered to navigate the rugged terrain, offers numerous pull-offs and viewpoints where travelers can pause to absorb the panoramic views and capture the breathtaking scenery.

Wildlife Encounters and Flora Diversity:

Independence Pass is not only a visual feast for the eyes but also a haven for wildlife enthusiasts and botanists. The surrounding wilderness is home to various species of wildlife, including marmots, pikas, and elusive mountain goats. Keep a keen eye, and you might spot these creatures as they navigate the rocky slopes or graze in the meadows.

During the summer months, the pass transforms into a vibrant tapestry of wildflowers. Blankets of colorful blooms, ranging from alpine forget-me-nots to Indian paintbrushes, adorn the landscape, creating a stunning contrast against the rocky backdrop. The diversity of flora is a testament to the resilience and adaptability of life at such high altitudes.

Historical Significance:

Beyond its natural wonders, Independence Pass boasts historical significance that adds depth to the journey. The pass derives its name from the Independence mining town, which thrived in the late 1800s during the Colorado Silver Boom. While the town is no longer standing, the echoes of its past resonate in the landscape, offering a glimpse into the challenges faced by early settlers and miners.

Glimpses of Twin Lakes:

As you approach the summit of Independence Pass, the landscape transitions once again, revealing the awe-inspiring Twin Lakes. These glacial lakes, nestled at the base of rugged peaks, reflect the surrounding mountains in their clear waters. Twin Lakes, flanked by dense forests, provide a serene contrast to the dramatic vistas experienced during the drive.

Tips for Travelers:

- Timing is Key: While Independence Pass is open seasonally, typically from late spring to early fall, it's crucial to check the road conditions before planning your trip. Winter snowfall can impact accessibility, so be sure to visit during the recommended months.
- Pack Accordingly: As you ascend to higher altitudes, temperatures may drop, even during the summer. Ensure you bring layers to stay comfortable and protect yourself from the elements.
- Take Your Time: The journey through Independence Pass is not one to be rushed. Allow ample time for stops at viewpoints, short hikes, and simply absorbing the grandeur of the surroundings.
- Photography Essentials: Don't forget your camera! Whether you're a professional photographer or just capturing memories, Independence Pass offers endless opportunities for stunning photographs.
- Respect Nature: Preserve the pristine environment by adhering to Leave No Trace principles. Respect wildlife from a distance and stay on designated paths to minimize human impact.

3.4 Aspen Art Museum

Nestled in the heart of the enchanting town of Aspen, the Aspen Art Museum stands as a cultural oasis, beckoning visitors to explore a world where artistic expression transcends boundaries. As part of the must-visit destinations in Aspen, the museum holds a distinctive position, offering a profound and enriching experience for tourists seeking to immerse themselves in the town's vibrant cultural scene.

History and Architecture

The Aspen Art Museum, established in 1979, has played a pivotal role in fostering creativity and artistic exploration in the region. Initially housed in a historic Victorian building, the museum underwent a transformative architectural makeover in 2014. The contemporary structure, designed by award-winning architect Shigeru Ban, not only serves as a testament to modern architectural brilliance but also as a canvas for the exhibitions it houses.

The new building, with its grand geometric design and expansive glass façade, provides a striking contrast to the surrounding mountain landscape. The intentional use of glass ensures that visitors are not only treated to captivating exhibits inside but also to panoramic views of Aspen and the surrounding mountains. This architectural feat has elevated the museum itself to a work of art, seamlessly integrating with the town's unique blend of natural beauty and cultural sophistication.

Exhibitions and Installations

The Aspen Art Museum prides itself on showcasing a diverse range of contemporary art from both emerging and established artists. The rotating exhibitions span various mediums, including painting, sculpture, photography, and multimedia installations. Tourists can expect a dynamic and ever-evolving lineup of exhibits that challenge perceptions, spark dialogue, and offer unique insights into the world of contemporary art.

One notable aspect of the museum is its commitment to presenting cutting-edge works by artists who push the boundaries of conventional artistic expression. The exhibits often delve into thought-provoking themes, inviting visitors to explore and interpret the art in a way that resonates personally. From solo exhibitions highlighting the work of a single artist to group shows that explore broader narratives, the Aspen Art Museum ensures a rich and engaging experience for art enthusiasts.

Educational Initiatives and Community Engagement

Beyond the galleries, the Aspen Art Museum is dedicated to fostering a deep connection with the community and nurturing the next generation of artists and art appreciators. The museum hosts a range of educational programs, workshops, and events designed to engage visitors of all ages. From guided tours that provide context to the exhibits to hands-on workshops that encourage artistic expression, the museum actively seeks to demystify contemporary art and make it accessible to everyone.

The commitment to education extends beyond the museum's physical walls. The museum collaborates with local schools, artists-in-residence, and cultural organizations to create a comprehensive cultural ecosystem. By doing so, it not only enhances the cultural vibrancy of Aspen but also contributes to the broader dialogue on the role of art in society.

Visitor Experience

Tourists visiting the Aspen Art Museum can expect an immersive and thought-provoking journey into the world of contemporary art. The museum's welcoming atmosphere, coupled with its commitment to accessibility, ensures that visitors of all backgrounds and levels of art expertise can engage with the exhibits on a meaningful level.

Upon entering the museum, visitors are greeted by knowledgeable and approachable staff who are passionate about sharing the stories behind the art. Guided tours, both scheduled and impromptu, provide valuable insights into the exhibits, allowing visitors to gain a deeper understanding of the artistic process and the context in which the works were created.

The museum's rooftop terrace, with its breathtaking views of Aspen's mountainous landscape, offers a unique space for reflection and appreciation. It has become a popular spot for visitors to pause and absorb the artistic and natural beauty that surrounds them.

Events and Cultural Offerings

In addition to its regular exhibitions, the Aspen Art Museum hosts a diverse array of events throughout the year. From artist talks and panel discussions to film screenings and live performances, the museum's calendar is filled with opportunities for cultural enrichment. These events not only complement the exhibits but also create a dynamic cultural hub that fosters dialogue and connection among visitors and the local community.

For tourists seeking a more in-depth experience, the museum often organizes special programs, including curator-led tours, allowing a behind-the-scenes look at the curation process. This insider perspective provides valuable insights into the thought and effort that goes into creating a cohesive and engaging exhibition.

Culmination of Art and Nature

One of the unique aspects of the Aspen Art Museum is its harmonious integration with the natural surroundings. The juxtaposition of the sleek, modern architecture against the backdrop of the Rocky Mountains creates a visual synergy that enhances the overall visitor experience. The museum's design, with its use of glass and open spaces, invites the outside in, blurring the boundaries between the curated art within and the natural beauty outside.

Visitors often find themselves captivated not only by the art on display but also by the interplay of light and shadow as the natural elements interact with the museum's architecture. This intentional design choice adds an extra layer of enchantment to the overall ambiance, making a visit to the Aspen Art Museum a truly immersive and multisensory experience.

Practical Information for Tourists

For tourists planning to visit the Aspen Art Museum, it's essential to check the museum's official website for up-to-date information on current exhibitions, opening hours, and any special events or programs. The museum is conveniently located in downtown Aspen, making it easily accessible for those exploring the town on foot.

Admission to the Aspen Art Museum is typically free, reflecting the institution's commitment to making art accessible to the widest possible audience. However, donations are encouraged to support the museum's ongoing efforts to provide engaging exhibitions, educational programs, and community outreach.

3.5 John Denver Sanctuary

Nestled within the heart of Aspen, the John Denver Sanctuary stands as a unique and tranquil destination that pays homage to the legendary musician, John Denver. For tourists visiting Aspen, this sanctuary is a must-visit, offering not only a serene natural environment but also a profound connection to the musical heritage that Denver left behind.

Location and Setting:

The John Denver Sanctuary is strategically located along the Roaring Fork River, within walking distance from downtown Aspen. This natural haven encompasses a beautiful six-acre park, providing an oasis of calm amidst the vibrant energy of the town. As tourists enter this sanctuary, they are greeted by the soothing sounds of the river, creating a harmonious backdrop for the tribute to one of America's most beloved folk musicians.

A Musical Tribute:

John Denver, known for hits like "Take Me Home, Country Roads" and "Rocky Mountain High," found inspiration in the natural beauty that surrounded Aspen. The sanctuary is a testament to this love affair between Denver and the Rockies. Visitors can explore the grounds adorned with lyrics from Denver's songs, engraved on rocks and boulders, creating a poetic ambiance that resonates with the spirit of his music.

Scenic Beauty and Natural Elements:

Beyond its musical tribute, the John Denver Sanctuary is a celebration of Aspen's stunning natural beauty. The sanctuary features meandering stone paths, vibrant flower gardens, and carefully placed boulders that invite contemplation. The Roaring Fork River flows gently, providing a soothing soundtrack to the visitor's experience. This combination of natural elements and artistic expressions creates a unique and immersive environment.

Contemplation Areas:

Scattered throughout the sanctuary are contemplation areas where visitors can pause, reflect, and connect with the surroundings. These serene spots offer breathtaking views of the surrounding mountains, providing a perfect setting for moments of quiet introspection. Whether sitting by the river or finding a secluded nook among the aspen trees, tourists can absorb the tranquility of the sanctuary.

Interactive Elements:

The John Denver Sanctuary goes beyond a passive tribute; it invites visitors to actively engage with the environment. The engraved lyrics on the rocks not only tell the story of Denver's connection to Aspen but also encourage a tactile and participatory experience. Tourists often find themselves tracing the words with their fingers, further immersing themselves in the lyrics that capture the essence of the Rocky Mountains.

Seasonal Variations:

One of the unique aspects of the sanctuary is its ever-changing landscape throughout the seasons. In spring and summer, vibrant wildflowers bloom, creating a burst of color against the greenery. Autumn transforms the sanctuary into a tapestry of gold as the aspen leaves change, and winter blankets the park in a serene layer of snow. Each season brings a new perspective, ensuring that return visits are equally enchanting.

Wildlife Encounters:

Aspen is not only a haven for humans but also a thriving ecosystem for wildlife. The John Denver Sanctuary provides an opportunity for tourists to observe local fauna in their natural habitat. Squirrels playfully dart among the trees, and birds add their melodies to the soundscape, creating a harmonious coexistence between nature and visitors.

Visitor Experience:

The sanctuary is designed to cater to a diverse range of visitors. Whether one seeks a peaceful escape from the hustle and bustle of the town or desires a deeper connection to John Denver's musical legacy, the sanctuary accommodates all. Families with children can enjoy a leisurely stroll, and music enthusiasts can find inspiration in the lyrics that surround them.

Accessibility and Amenities:

For the convenience of tourists, the John Denver Sanctuary is easily accessible from downtown Aspen. The sanctuary is a short walk from popular shopping and dining areas, allowing visitors to seamlessly incorporate it into their Aspen itinerary. Additionally, well-maintained paths and seating areas make the sanctuary accessible to individuals of all ages and mobility levels.

Events and Gatherings:

The John Denver Sanctuary serves not only as a tourist attraction but also as a venue for events and gatherings. Local performances, musical events, and even small weddings take place in this natural amphitheater. The sanctuary provides a unique backdrop for celebrations, adding an extra layer of charm to special occasions.

Preservation and Conservation:

As a testament to Aspen's commitment to environmental sustainability, the John Denver Sanctuary is maintained with a focus on conservation. Efforts are made to preserve the natural integrity of the site, ensuring that future generations can continue to enjoy this sanctuary as a harmonious blend of nature and culture.

3.6 Aspen Music Festival and School

Nestled amid the picturesque landscapes of Aspen, Colorado, the Aspen Music Festival and School stands as a cultural oasis, inviting music enthusiasts from around the world to immerse themselves in a symphony of artistic excellence. This renowned institution not only captivates with its breathtaking mountain backdrop but also resonates with the melodies of classical and contemporary music, creating an unparalleled experience for both performers and audience members alike.

A Pinnacle of Musical Excellence

At the heart of Aspen's cultural scene, the Aspen Music Festival and School has been a beacon for musical excellence since its inception in 1949. Set against the backdrop of the Elk Mountain Range, this annual celebration of the arts attracts world-class musicians, aspiring performers, and avid listeners who gather to revel in the magic of live music.

The Summer Festival: A Melodic Extravaganza

The crown jewel of the Aspen Music Festival and School is undoubtedly its summer festival, a musical extravaganza that unfolds over eight weeks, typically from late June to August. During this time, the charming mountain town of Aspen transforms into a haven for classical music enthusiasts, with a diverse array of performances, masterclasses, and educational programs.

Concerts Amidst Nature's Grandeur

One of the unique aspects of the Aspen Music Festival is its venue selection. Concerts are not confined to traditional halls; instead, they resonate in the open air, allowing attendees to enjoy performances amidst the natural grandeur of Aspen. The Benedict Music Tent, with its striking architecture, becomes a focal point for symphony concerts, showcasing the synergy between human artistry and the awe-inspiring beauty of the surrounding mountains.

Masterclasses by Virtuosos

The festival's allure extends beyond the audience to include aspiring musicians, as the Aspen Music School provides an immersive learning experience. Masterclasses conducted by virtuosos offer students a rare opportunity to refine their skills under the guidance of some of the most accomplished musicians in the world. These intimate sessions foster a unique mentorship dynamic, contributing to the festival's reputation as a nurturing ground for emerging talent.

Diverse Repertoire and Performers

The Aspen Music Festival and School takes pride in its commitment to diversity, both in terms of repertoire and performers. Concert programs span a wide spectrum, featuring everything from classical masterpieces to contemporary compositions. The roster of performers includes seasoned professionals, faculty members, and the bright young stars of tomorrow, creating a dynamic and inclusive musical environment.

Aspen Conducting Academy: Shaping Future Maestros

For those with aspirations of standing on the conductor's podium, the Aspen Conducting Academy offers a transformative experience. This esteemed program provides conductors with the opportunity to refine their skills, collaborate with orchestras, and receive guidance from experienced mentors. The result is a cadre of emerging maestros who contribute to the rich tapestry of classical music.

Collaborations with Renowned Artists

The festival's commitment to artistic collaboration is evident in its partnerships with internationally acclaimed artists. From renowned conductors and soloists to esteemed composers, the Aspen Music Festival brings together luminaries who share their expertise and passion with both students and the appreciative audience.

Aspen Opera Theater and VocalARTS: The Human Voice in Harmony

Recognizing the power of the human voice, the Aspen Music Festival features the Aspen Opera Theater and VocalARTS program. This program focuses on operatic and vocal training, offering aspiring singers a platform to refine their craft. Performances range from beloved operatic classics to innovative contemporary works, showcasing the versatility of the human voice.

Beyond the Concert Hall: Music in the Streets

The influence of the Aspen Music Festival extends beyond the confines of traditional concert halls. Aspen's streets come alive with the sounds of music during the festival, as pop-up performances, street musicians, and impromptu jam sessions add an extra layer of vibrancy to the town's atmosphere. This integration of music into the fabric of daily life creates a unique and immersive experience for both visitors and residents.

Educational Outreach Programs: Inspiring the Next Generation

An integral part of the Aspen Music Festival and School's mission is its commitment to educational outreach. Through various programs, including concerts for young audiences, music education initiatives in schools, and community engagement events, the festival strives to inspire the next generation of music lovers and performers. These efforts ensure that the transformative power of music reaches beyond the festival grounds and into the hearts of the broader community.

Planning Your Visit to the Aspen Music Festival and School

If you're planning to experience the Aspen Music Festival and School, careful consideration of the festival schedule is essential. The summer program typically includes a diverse range of concerts, recitals, and special events. Tickets can be purchased for individual performances or as part of subscription packages, allowing you to tailor your experience based on your musical preferences.

Additionally, consider exploring Aspen's broader cultural and recreational offerings. The town boasts a thriving arts scene, boutique shopping, exquisite dining options, and outdoor activities that complement the cultural immersion provided by the music festival.

3.7 Aspen Highlands: Thrills and Panoramic Vistas

Nestled within the majestic embrace of the Colorado Rockies, Aspen Highlands stands as a pinnacle of adventure and natural beauty. This segment of our guide delves into the allure of Aspen Highlands, offering insights into the thrills it presents and the panoramic vistas that await every visitor.

Winter Wonderland: Skiing Extravaganza

Aspen Highlands is renowned as a winter wonderland that beckons skiing and snowboarding enthusiasts from across the globe. The terrain here is not for the faint of heart; it caters to those seeking an adrenaline-fueled descent down challenging slopes. The steep and varied runs make Aspen Highlands a favorite among expert skiers, offering a mix of tree-lined glades, groomed trails, and thrilling moguls.

Panoramic Views from the Summit

The true jewel of Aspen Highlands lies at its summit. Ascending to the pinnacle is an adventure in itself, and the reward is unparalleled panoramic views that stretch across the Elk Mountains and beyond. The Maroon Bells, with their iconic twin peaks, grace the horizon, creating a breathtaking backdrop that epitomizes the rugged beauty of the Colorado Rockies. The sense of accomplishment upon reaching the summit is matched only by the awe-inspiring scenery that unfolds before your eyes.

Highland Bowl: A Bucket List Experience

For those seeking the ultimate skiing adventure, the Highland Bowl is a bucket list experience at Aspen Highlands. This legendary bowl offers steep and challenging terrain that pushes even the most seasoned skiers to their limits. The reward for conquering the bowl is not just the thrill of the descent but also the sense of conquering a formidable peak, standing tall at over 12,000 feet.

The Cloud Nine Alpine Bistro: Culinary Delights at Altitude

After an exhilarating day on the slopes, Aspen Highlands provides a unique culinary experience at The Cloud Nine Alpine Bistro. Perched at an elevation of 10,740 feet, this renowned restaurant offers not only gourmet cuisine but also breathtaking views of the surrounding mountains. It's an opportunity to savor delectable dishes while surrounded by the crisp mountain air and the stunning alpine landscape.

Summer Hiking Adventures

While Aspen Highlands is celebrated for its winter offerings, the summer months bring a different kind of magic. The snow retreats, revealing a network of hiking trails that cater to a spectrum of skill levels. From leisurely walks through wildflower-strewn meadows to challenging hikes leading to the summit, summer at Aspen Highlands unveils a vibrant alpine ecosystem waiting to be explored.

Maroon Creek Road Scenic Drive

Even if you're not an avid hiker or skier, Aspen Highlands has a treat in store for you. The Maroon Creek Road Scenic Drive is a leisurely journey that allows you to soak in the grandeur of the surrounding landscape from the comfort of your vehicle. As you wind along the road, the Maroon Bells loom majestically, providing ample opportunities for stops and photo-worthy moments.

Unforgettable Apres-Ski Atmosphere

No visit to Aspen Highlands is complete without immersing yourself in the après-ski atmosphere. The base area comes alive with the contagious energy of fellow adventurers sharing stories of their day on the slopes. Cozy up by the fire pits, enjoy live music, and relish the camaraderie that defines the après-ski culture in Aspen Highlands.

Insider Tips for Aspen Highlands Exploration

For an optimal experience at Aspen Highlands, consider these insider tips:

- Early Mornings for Fresh Tracks: If you're an avid skier, hitting the slopes early ensures you carve through pristine, untouched snow, especially in Highland Bowl.
- Scenic Photography Spots: Capture the magic of Aspen Highlands by exploring designated scenic viewpoints along the trails and at the summit.
- Highland Bowl Orientation Session: If you're attempting the Highland Bowl for the first time, joining an orientation session can provide valuable

insights and enhance your safety on this challenging terrain.

- Dress in Layers: Aspen's mountain weather can be unpredictable. Dressing in layers ensures you stay comfortable and prepared for changing conditions throughout the day.

3.8 Smuggler Mountain Trail

Nestled within the embrace of the Rocky Mountains, Aspen unveils a myriad of outdoor adventures, and among them, the Smuggler Mountain Trail stands as a testament to the region's natural splendor and hiking prowess. For tourists seeking a blend of tranquility, exercise, and breathtaking vistas, the Smuggler Mountain Trail is an absolute must-visit.

Location and Access:

The trailhead for the Smuggler Mountain Trail is conveniently located near downtown Aspen, making it easily accessible for visitors staying in the heart of the town. A short drive or a brisk walk from most accommodations in Aspen brings you to the trailhead, ready to embark on a journey through nature's wonders.

The trail is open year-round, providing different experiences with each season. During the warmer months, from late spring to early fall, hikers can enjoy blooming wildflowers, lush vegetation, and warmer temperatures. In the winter, the trail transforms into a snowy wonderland, inviting snowshoers and winter hikers to revel in a serene landscape blanketed in white.

The Trail Experience:

The Smuggler Mountain Trail is renowned for offering a perfect balance between accessibility for casual hikers and challenges for those seeking a more vigorous workout. The initial segment of the trail is wide and well-maintained, making it suitable for families, beginners, or anyone looking for a leisurely stroll.

As you ascend, the trail meanders through groves of Aspen trees, adding a touch of enchantment to the journey. The rhythmic rustling of leaves in the breeze creates a serene soundtrack, providing a stark contrast to the bustling energy of downtown Aspen just below.

For those craving a more strenuous adventure, the trail gradually becomes steeper, presenting a moderate incline that elevates the heart rate and provides a satisfying workout. Hiking boots and comfortable attire are recommended, allowing visitors to fully appreciate the varying terrain.

Flora and Fauna:

One of the unique features of the Smuggler Mountain Trail is its diverse ecosystem. Aspen trees, with their distinctive white bark, dominate the lower portions of the trail, creating a visually striking landscape. As you ascend, the vegetation changes, offering encounters with coniferous trees, wildflowers, and mountain shrubs.

Keep an eye out for the local wildlife that calls Smuggler Mountain home. Squirrels, mule deer, and a variety of bird species are common sights. Lucky hikers may even catch a glimpse of a majestic elk or a curious fox, adding an element of wildlife observation to the hiking experience.

Panoramic Views from the Summit:

The ultimate reward for conquering the Smuggler Mountain Trail is the panoramic spectacle that awaits at the summit. As you reach the top, a breathtaking 360-degree view unfolds, showcasing the entire Roaring Fork Valley, Aspen Mountain, and the surrounding peaks of the Elk Mountain Range.

The town of Aspen below appears like a miniature village nestled amidst the sprawling wilderness. The sight is particularly enchanting during sunrise or sunset when the sky is painted in hues of pink, orange, and purple, casting a warm glow over the landscape.

Photographers, both amateur and professional, find the summit of Smuggler Mountain to be an ideal vantage point for capturing the beauty of Aspen and its natural surroundings. The play of light and shadow on the mountains, coupled with the changing colors of the seasons, provides an ever-evolving canvas for creative exploration.

Hiking Tips and Considerations:

- Pack Essentials: Ensure you have essentials such as water, snacks, a hat, sunscreen, and a camera. The unpredictable mountain weather may warrant an extra layer or a light jacket even in the warmer months.
- Trail Etiquette: Respect the trail and fellow hikers. Yield to uphill hikers, and keep dogs on a leash to

preserve the natural environment and ensure a positive experience for everyone.

- Trail Conditions: Check trail conditions before embarking on your hike, especially during the winter months. While the trail is maintained, winter weather may require additional precautions such as traction devices for shoes.
- Leave No Trace: Follow the principles of Leave No Trace. Pack out all trash, stay on designated trails, and avoid disturbing wildlife to help preserve the pristine beauty of Smuggler Mountain.

3.9 Woody Creek Tavern

For tourists seeking an authentic taste of Aspen's culture, culinary delights, and a touch of local history, a visit to Woody Creek Tavern is an absolute must.

1. Location and Setting

Woody Creek Tavern is situated approximately 12 miles northwest of downtown Aspen, making it a scenic drive through the picturesque countryside. The tavern is surrounded by the stunning beauty of the Rocky Mountains, creating a rustic yet inviting atmosphere that reflects the essence of Aspen's mountain lifestyle.

2. A Historical Landmark

Established in 1980, Woody Creek Tavern has earned its place as a historical landmark in the region. The tavern has a rich history, having served as a gathering place for locals, artists, writers, and even celebrities over the years. The walls are adorned with memorabilia, photographs, and artifacts, creating a visual timeline that tells the story of Woody Creek and its significance in the Aspen community.

3. An Encounter with Aspen's Creative Spirit

One of the unique aspects of Woody Creek Tavern is its connection to the creative spirit that defines Aspen. This establishment has been a favorite haunt for writers and artists, including the legendary Hunter S. Thompson, who frequented the tavern. As you step inside, you'll feel the echoes of Aspen's bohemian past, providing an opportunity to immerse yourself in the cultural currents that have shaped the town.

4. Culinary Delights with Local Flair

Woody Creek Tavern is renowned for its diverse menu that reflects the culinary flair of the region. From hearty American classics to inventive dishes, the tavern caters to a range of tastes. Visitors can savor mouthwatering burgers, flavorful Mexican cuisine, and fresh salads made from locally sourced ingredients. The menu is a testament to Aspen's commitment to offering a culinary experience that mirrors its vibrant and diverse community.

5. Signature Drinks and Libations

No visit to Woody Creek Tavern is complete without indulging in its signature drinks and libations. The tavern boasts an impressive selection of craft beers, cocktails, and an extensive wine list. Whether you're looking to unwind after a day of exploring Aspen or to toast to new memories, the welcoming atmosphere of the tavern sets the stage for an enjoyable and convivial experience.

6. Community Gathering Spot

Woody Creek Tavern is more than just a restaurant; it is a community gathering spot where locals and visitors come together to share stories, laughter, and a sense of camaraderie. The friendly and laid-back ambiance makes it an ideal place to strike up conversations with locals, learning more about the town's hidden gems and insider tips.

7. Live Music and Events

To enhance the overall experience, Woody Creek Tavern regularly hosts live music and events. The intimate setting provides the perfect backdrop for local musicians to showcase their talent, creating a lively and entertaining atmosphere. Check the schedule to see if your visit aligns with one of these performances, adding a musical touch to your Aspen experience.

8. The Outdoor Patio Experience

In the warmer months, Woody Creek Tavern's outdoor patio becomes a coveted spot for patrons. Surrounded by the natural beauty of Aspen, the patio offers an al fresco dining experience like no other. Breathe in the crisp mountain air as you enjoy your meal and soak in the serene surroundings.

9. Visitor Tips and Recommendations

For those planning to visit Woody Creek Tavern, consider the following tips:

- Peak Hours: The tavern can get busy, especially during peak hours, so it's advisable to plan your visit during off-peak times to ensure a more relaxed dining experience.

- Local Recommendations: Don't hesitate to ask the friendly staff for recommendations. Locals often have their favorite dishes and drinks, and the staff is more than happy to guide you through the menu.
- Celebrate Local Events: Check if your visit coincides with any local events or festivals. Woody Creek Tavern often hosts special events, providing an opportunity to immerse yourself in the vibrant cultural scene of Aspen.
- Transportation: Consider transportation options, especially if you plan to indulge in the tavern's diverse drink offerings. Many visitors opt for shuttle services or designated drivers to ensure a safe and enjoyable evening.

10. How to Get There

Woody Creek Tavern is easily accessible from Aspen by car. Visitors can take a scenic drive, enjoying the landscapes that surround Aspen. If you prefer not to drive, shuttle services are available, providing a convenient and stress-free way to reach this iconic destination.

3.10 Aspen Center for Environmental Studies (ACES)

As a must-visit destination, ACES offers a unique blend of educational programs, immersive experiences, and breathtaking surroundings that make it an integral part of any Aspen itinerary.

1. The Gateway to Environmental Education:

Located on the banks of the Roaring Fork River, ACES serves as a gateway to environmental education. Its mission is to inspire a greater sense of environmental stewardship through hands-on learning and engagement. Whether you're a seasoned naturalist or someone taking their first steps into the world of ecology, ACES provides a rich learning environment.

2. Interactive Exhibits and Educational Displays:

The Aspen Center for Environmental Studies features a range of interactive exhibits and educational displays designed to unravel the secrets of the local ecosystem. From geological formations to the intricacies of flora and fauna, these exhibits cater to visitors of all ages, making it a family-friendly destination.

3. Guided Nature Walks:

ACES offers guided nature walks led by knowledgeable naturalists. These walks traverse the surrounding areas, providing insights into the diverse ecosystems, plant life, and wildlife that call Aspen home. It's an excellent opportunity to gain a deeper understanding of the region's natural balance while enjoying the fresh mountain air.

4. Birding Adventures:

For bird enthusiasts, ACES organizes birding adventures that take participants to birding hotspots in the Aspen area. With over 300 bird species identified in the Roaring Fork Valley, this experience offers a chance to spot various avian species and appreciate the region's biodiversity.

5. Rock Bottom Ranch: A Living Classroom:

ACES extends its educational reach to Rock Bottom Ranch, a living classroom situated along the Roaring Fork River. Here, visitors can explore sustainable agriculture practices, interact with farm animals, and learn about the vital connection between food production and environmental health.

6. Wildlife Viewing Stations:

Strategically positioned wildlife viewing stations within the ACES grounds allow visitors to observe local fauna in their natural habitats. Whether it's catching a glimpse of a red fox or spotting a majestic bald eagle, these stations offer a serene and respectful way to connect with the diverse wildlife of Aspen.

7. Educational Programs for All Ages:

ACES hosts a wide array of educational programs catering to different age groups. From children's nature camps to adult workshops, these programs cover topics ranging from astronomy to sustainable living practices. This diversity ensures that everyone, regardless of age or background, can find a program that resonates with their interests.

8. Naturalist-led Workshops:

Engage in naturalist-led workshops that delve into specific aspects of the environment. These workshops cover topics such as botany, ecology, and wildlife tracking. Led by experts in their fields, these sessions provide an in-depth exploration of Aspen's unique ecosystems.

9. ACES Eco-Tours:

For those seeking a comprehensive exploration of the region, ACES offers eco-tours that traverse diverse landscapes. These tours may include visits to alpine meadows, pristine forests, and serene wetlands, allowing participants to witness the variety of ecosystems that thrive in the Aspen area.

10. Educational Outreach and Community Involvement:

ACES is deeply committed to community involvement and educational outreach. The center collaborates with schools, local organizations, and the broader community to promote environmental literacy and sustainability. Visitors can witness the positive impact ACES has on shaping a more ecologically conscious community.

11. ACF: Aspen Community Foundation Partnership:

In collaboration with the Aspen Community Foundation (ACF), ACES contributes to initiatives aimed at preserving the natural beauty of Aspen and fostering a sense of environmental responsibility. The partnership emphasizes the importance of community-driven efforts in preserving the region's ecological integrity.

12. The James H. Smith Rock and Alpine Garden:

Nature enthusiasts will appreciate the James H. Smith Rock and Alpine Garden, a gem within the ACES premises. This meticulously curated garden showcases a diverse collection of alpine flora, emphasizing the delicate balance and adaptability of plant life in high-altitude environments.

3.11 Hunter Creek Trail

One of Aspen's hidden gems, the Hunter Creek Trail, is a nature lover's paradise, offering an immersive experience in the heart of the Colorado Rockies. This enchanting trail is not only a favorite among locals but also a must-visit for tourists seeking a genuine connection with Aspen's pristine wilderness.

Location and Accessibility

Nestled just a short distance from downtown Aspen, the Hunter Creek Trailhead is conveniently accessible, making it an ideal escape for those looking to immerse themselves in nature without venturing too far from the town's amenities. Visitors can easily locate the trailhead near the base of Smuggler Mountain, providing a seamless transition from the vibrant town to the tranquility of the trail.

Scenic Beauty and Natural Diversity

As you embark on the Hunter Creek Trail, the first thing that captures your attention is the lush, dense foliage that lines the path. Towering pine trees create a canopy overhead, filtering the sunlight and casting a gentle glow on the trail below. The sound of a babbling creek accompanies you, adding a soothing soundtrack to your hike.

The trail's natural diversity is a highlight, with each turn revealing new landscapes. From open meadows adorned with wildflowers to dense aspen groves that shimmer in the sunlight, Hunter Creek Trail showcases the rich tapestry of flora native to the region. During the fall, the aspen trees transform into a symphony of gold and amber, creating a breathtaking contrast against the evergreen backdrop.

Trail Difficulty and Options

Hunter Creek Trail caters to a wide range of hikers, from casual strollers to avid trekking enthusiasts. The lower section of the trail is relatively flat and well-maintained, making it accessible to families and those seeking a leisurely walk. As you ascend, the trail becomes more challenging, rewarding hikers with elevated views of the surrounding mountains.

For a shorter hike, visitors can explore the lower portions of the trail, which still provide a taste of the area's natural beauty. Alternatively, those seeking a more rigorous adventure can continue the ascent, eventually reaching higher elevations and panoramic vistas that showcase the grandeur of the Elk Mountains.

Wildlife Encounters

Nature enthusiasts will appreciate the opportunities for wildlife encounters along Hunter Creek Trail. Keep your eyes peeled for native species such as mule deer, elk, and various bird species. The tranquil setting provides a chance to observe these creatures in their natural habitat, adding an element of excitement to your hiking experience.

Picnic Spots and Relaxation Areas

Strategic clearings along the trail offer perfect spots for picnics or simply unwinding amid nature's embrace. Pack a picnic and take advantage of these designated areas to savor the fresh mountain air and recharge before continuing your journey. The serene surroundings create an ideal backdrop for moments of relaxation and reflection.

Historical Points of Interest

As you traverse the Hunter Creek Trail, you'll encounter remnants of Aspen's mining history. The remnants of old cabins and mining structures provide a glimpse into the area's past, adding an intriguing layer to the trail's narrative. Interpretive signs along the way offer insights into the significance of these historical features, creating a blend of outdoor adventure and cultural exploration.

Seasonal Considerations

Hunter Creek Trail is a year-round destination, each season offering a unique and captivating experience. In the spring and summer, the trail comes alive with blooming wildflowers and vibrant foliage. Autumn transforms the landscape into a canvas of warm hues, making it an excellent time for photographers and nature enthusiasts. Winter blankets the trail in snow, turning it into a peaceful, snow-covered haven for those seeking a winter wonderland experience.

Trail Etiquette and Conservation Efforts

As you traverse Hunter Creek Trail, it's essential to adhere to trail etiquette and conservation principles. Stay on designated paths, respect wildlife, and pack out any waste to preserve the pristine beauty of this natural haven. Aspen's commitment to sustainability is reflected in the conservation efforts undertaken to maintain the trail and its surroundings.

Guided Tours and Interpretive Programs

For those who prefer a more guided experience, Aspen offers guided tours and interpretive programs for Hunter Creek Trail. Knowledgeable guides share insights into the flora, fauna, and history of the area, enhancing the overall hiking experience. These programs provide a deeper understanding of Aspen's natural heritage while ensuring a safe and enjoyable journey for all participants.

3.12 Aspen Recreation Center (ARC)

This multifaceted facility offers a diverse array of activities and amenities, making it a must-visit destination for those seeking both indoor and outdoor adventures.

1. Facilities at a Glance:

The Aspen Recreation Center, situated on Maroon Creek Road, boasts state-of-the-art facilities catering to various interests and age groups.

The complex includes a full-size ice rink, a spacious swimming pool, a well-equipped fitness center, and numerous recreational spaces for both individual and group activities.

2. Ice Skating Extravaganza:

The highlight of ARC during the winter months is undoubtedly its full-size ice rink. Whether you're a seasoned skater or trying it for the first time, the rink provides a perfect setting for gliding gracefully or engaging in a spirited game of ice hockey.

Families can enjoy quality time together on the ice, creating cherished memories amidst the backdrop of snow-capped mountains.

3. Invigorating Swimming Experience:

The indoor swimming pool at ARC offers a refreshing escape, especially during the colder months. Take a dip in the heated pool or enjoy a leisurely swim, surrounded by large windows that frame panoramic views of the surrounding mountains.

Families with children will appreciate the separate kiddie pool, ensuring a safe and enjoyable aquatic experience for the little ones.

4. Fitness Center for Health Enthusiasts:

The Aspen Recreation Center caters to health enthusiasts with its well-equipped fitness center. Whether you prefer cardiovascular workouts, strength training, or group fitness classes, ARC provides a welcoming environment for achieving your fitness goals.

State-of-the-art equipment, experienced trainers, and a supportive atmosphere make the fitness center an essential stop for those prioritizing health and wellness during their Aspen visit.

5. Varied Recreational Spaces:

ARC extends its appeal beyond ice and water activities. The center features multiple recreational spaces, including basketball courts, a climbing wall, and a racquetball court.

Sports enthusiasts can engage in friendly competitions, while those seeking a bit of adventure can try their hand at climbing the indoor rock wall for a thrilling and fulfilling experience.

6. Year-Round Events and Programs:

One of the unique aspects of ARC is its commitment to hosting a variety of events and programs throughout the year. From fitness challenges to family-oriented activities, there's always something happening at the center.

Tourists can check the event calendar to align their visit with special programs, ensuring an even more dynamic and engaging experience at ARC.

7. Kid-Friendly Amenities:

Traveling with children? ARC is an ideal destination for families. The center provides a supervised Kids Club, allowing parents to enjoy their chosen activities while ensuring that the little ones are entertained and cared for in a safe environment.

The family-friendly atmosphere extends to the entire facility, making ARC a welcoming space for visitors of all ages.

8. ARC in Summer:

While ARC is renowned for its winter offerings, the center seamlessly transitions into a haven of summer activities. The outdoor facilities come alive with possibilities, including tennis courts, a skate park, and expansive green spaces for picnics and relaxation.

Families, in particular, can appreciate the diversity of options, ensuring that the fun doesn't pause with the changing seasons.

9. Accessibility and Convenience:

Located conveniently near downtown Aspen, ARC is easily accessible for tourists staying in the area. The facility provides ample parking, and shuttle services are often available, ensuring that visitors can reach the center without hassle.

The proximity of ARC to other Aspen attractions makes it a flexible addition to any itinerary, allowing tourists to seamlessly incorporate a few hours of recreation into their exploration of the town.

10. Community Engagement and Local Flavor:

ARC is not just a recreation center; it's a hub for community engagement. Visitors can witness the local spirit as residents and tourists come together to enjoy the various amenities.

Engaging with locals and participating in the center's activities provides an authentic Aspen experience, allowing tourists to immerse themselves in the vibrant local culture.

3.13 Ashcroft Ghost Town

Tucked away in the serene mountains surrounding Aspen, the Ashcroft Ghost Town stands as a poignant reminder of Aspen's storied past. As you embark on your journey to explore this well-preserved relic of the silver mining era, you'll find yourself immersed in a captivating narrative that unfolds with every step.

History Beckons:

Ashcroft was born during the late 19th century, a bustling silver mining town with aspirations as high as the peaks that cradled it. Founded in 1880, the town quickly thrived, boasting a post office, saloons, hotels, and even a schoolhouse. At its peak, Ashcroft was home to over 2,000 residents and seemed destined for greatness.

The promise of wealth drawn from the silver mines, however, was short-lived. By the turn of the century, the mines were exhausted, and the once-vibrant town faced a rapid decline. Today, Ashcroft stands frozen in time, its weathered buildings and vacant streets echoing the whispers of a bygone era.

Preserving the Past:

As you wander through the ghost town, you'll witness the careful preservation efforts that have allowed Ashcroft to maintain its authenticity. The ghost town was designated a historic site in the 1970s, ensuring that its structures and stories would be safeguarded for future generations.

Buildings like the Blue Mirror Saloon, the View Hotel, and the Miners Union Hall remain standing, offering a glimpse into the daily lives of the hardworking miners and their families. The Ghost Town Stabilization Project has been instrumental in maintaining these structures, allowing visitors to step back in time and connect with Aspen's fascinating history.

The Blue Mirror Saloon: A Relic of Revelry:

At the heart of Ashcroft lies the Blue Mirror Saloon, a gathering place that once echoed with the laughter and camaraderie of miners seeking respite from the challenges of their daily toil. The saloon's name is said to have originated from its distinctive blue mirrored interior, an extravagant touch for its time. Today, the saloon serves as a portal to the past, where you can almost hear the clinking of glasses and lively conversations that filled the air over a century ago.

The View Hotel: Witness to Changing Fortunes:

Overlooking the town, the View Hotel stands as a silent witness to the changing fortunes of Ashcroft. Originally constructed as the Windsor Hotel in 1883, it catered to the town's elite, offering a luxurious escape from the harsh realities of mining life. However, with the decline of the silver industry, the hotel fell into disuse, mirroring the fate of the town itself. Visitors can stand on its porch and absorb the sweeping views of the surrounding mountains, contemplating the passage of time.

Miners Union Hall: A Testament to Solidarity:

The Miners Union Hall reflects the spirit of solidarity that defined the mining community. Constructed in 1885, it served as a gathering place for miners to discuss labor issues and socialize. The hall hosted dances, meetings, and even theatrical performances, providing a sense of community amidst the challenges of mining life. Today, its weathered facade stands as a testament to the resilience of those who once called Ashcroft home.

Visiting Tips and Considerations:

When planning your visit to Ashcroft Ghost Town, consider the following tips to enhance your experience:

- Guided Tours: Opt for a guided tour to gain deeper insights into the history and stories behind the ghost town. Knowledgeable guides provide context to the structures and share anecdotes that bring the past to life.
- Seasonal Considerations: Ashcroft is open to visitors during the summer months when the weather is more accommodating. However, it's advisable to check for any seasonal closures or special events that may affect your visit.
- Comfortable Footwear: Wear sturdy and comfortable footwear, as you'll be exploring uneven terrain. The pathways may include gravel, dirt, and remnants of historic structures.
- Photography Opportunities: Bring your camera to capture the hauntingly beautiful scenes of the ghost town against the backdrop of the surrounding mountains. The interplay of light and shadows on the weathered buildings creates a photographer's paradise.
- Respectful Exploration: While exploring Ashcroft, be mindful of the historic nature of the site. Refrain from touching or entering the structures, as they are fragile and need to be preserved for future generations.

3.14 Anderson Ranch Arts Center

Introduction to Anderson Ranch Arts Center: A Haven for Creativity

Anderson Ranch Arts Center, located in the picturesque Snowmass Village, is more than just an art institution; it's a haven for creativity that has been nurturing artistic talents since its inception. Established in 1966, the center has become a vital part of Aspen's cultural landscape, offering a space where artists from diverse backgrounds converge to explore, create, and share their passion for the arts.

The Setting: Where Nature and Art Converge

One of the unique aspects of Anderson Ranch is its stunning natural setting. Surrounded by the majestic peaks of the Colorado Rockies, the center provides artists and visitors alike with an inspiring backdrop that enhances the creative process. The combination of crisp mountain air, the soothing sounds of nature, and the ever-changing colors of the landscape creates an atmosphere conducive to artistic exploration and expression.

Workshops and Programs: A Canvas of Possibilities

At the heart of Anderson Ranch's mission is its commitment to education and artistic development. The center offers a diverse array of workshops, classes, and residency programs catering to individuals of all skill levels and artistic interests. From traditional painting and sculpture to cutting-edge digital media and new media arts, Anderson Ranch provides a canvas of possibilities for artists to explore and expand their craft.

Visitors have the opportunity to witness the creative process firsthand as they stroll through the studios and workshops, where artists engage in the act of making, experimenting, and refining their works. The vibrant energy that permeates the center is a testament to the dedication of both emerging and established artists who converge at Anderson Ranch to share their expertise and passion for the arts.

Exhibitions and Galleries: Showcasing Artistic Excellence

Anderson Ranch Arts Center is not only a place of creation but also a venue for the appreciation of art. The center hosts a rotating series of exhibitions featuring works by resident artists, faculty members, and invited guest artists. These exhibitions offer a glimpse into the diverse and dynamic world of contemporary art, spanning a wide range of mediums and styles.

The galleries at Anderson Ranch serve as spaces for dialogue, where visitors can engage with the artists and gain insights into the inspirations behind their creations. Whether you are a seasoned art enthusiast or someone new to the world of contemporary art, the exhibitions at Anderson Ranch provide an enriching and immersive experience.

Artist Residencies: Fostering a Community of Creativity

Anderson Ranch Arts Center takes pride in its artist-in-residence program, which attracts talents from around the globe. These residencies provide artists with the time, space, and resources to focus on their creative endeavors, free from the distractions of everyday life. The result is a dynamic and collaborative community of artists who bring diverse perspectives and skills to the Ranch.

Visitors to Anderson Ranch have the opportunity to engage with resident artists, attend open studios, and gain insights into the artistic process. This interactive and communal aspect of the center fosters a sense of connection between artists and visitors, creating an environment where ideas flow freely, and creativity knows no bounds.

Community Engagement: Art for All

Anderson Ranch Arts Center is deeply committed to making art accessible to all members of the community. The center hosts a variety of events, lectures, and outreach programs designed to engage both residents and visitors in the world of art. From family-friendly art activities to thought-provoking discussions on the intersection of art and society, Anderson Ranch strives to be a hub of cultural enrichment for Aspen and beyond.

The commitment to community engagement extends to educational programs for local schools, ensuring that the next generation of artists and art enthusiasts have the opportunity to explore their creativity under the guidance of experienced instructors.

Planning Your Visit: Practical Information

If you're inspired to include Anderson Ranch Arts Center in your Aspen itinerary, here are some practical details to enhance your visit:

- Location: Anderson Ranch is situated in Snowmass Village, approximately eight miles from downtown Aspen. The address is 5263 Owl Creek Road, Snowmass Village, CO 81615.
- Visitor Hours: The center is open to visitors during specific hours, and it's advisable to check the official website for the latest information on exhibition schedules, workshops, and events.
- Tours: Guided tours of the studios and galleries are available, providing in-depth insights into the creative process and the history of Anderson Ranch Arts Center.
- Workshops and Classes: If you're feeling inspired, consider participating in one of the workshops or classes offered by the center. These experiences allow you to tap into your own artistic potential under the guidance of experienced instructors.
- Events Calendar: To make the most of your visit, check the events calendar on the official website. Anderson Ranch hosts a variety of events throughout the year, including artist talks, exhibitions, and community programs.

3.15 The Ute Trail
Overview of the Ute Trail

The Ute Trail is a captivating hiking trail that winds its way through the Aspen high country, showcasing the untamed beauty of the Elk Mountain Range. This trail is not just a physical excursion; it's a journey into the heart of the Rocky Mountains, revealing the rich biodiversity and geological wonders that define the Aspen landscape.

Trailhead and Access Points

The trailhead for the Ute Trail is conveniently located on the eastern edge of Aspen, near the Aspen Mountain Gondola. This accessibility makes it a favorite among both novice hikers and seasoned adventurers. The trail's moderate difficulty level caters to a broad range of hikers, allowing everyone to partake in the wonders that unfold along the Ute Trail.

Scenic Beauty Along the Trail

Embarking on the Ute Trail is like stepping into a postcard-worthy landscape. As you ascend, the trail offers sweeping panoramas of the Roaring Fork Valley, with Aspen's quaint town nestled below. The Maroon Bells, standing proudly in the distance, add a touch of majesty to the scene, creating a picturesque backdrop that will undoubtedly find a permanent place in your memory.

The trail meanders through dense forests adorned with quaking aspen trees, which shimmer like gold in the fall. Wildflowers carpet the meadows during the warmer months, creating a vibrant tapestry of colors against the backdrop of the rugged mountains. The Ute Trail is a photographer's delight, capturing the essence of Aspen's natural beauty in every frame.

Historical Significance of the Ute Trail

Beyond its scenic allure, the Ute Trail is steeped in historical significance. The Ute people, indigenous to the region, once traversed these lands, leaving behind a cultural legacy that echoes through the ages. As you hike, imagine the footsteps of those who came before, adding a profound layer to your experience.

The trail takes its name from the Ute Indians, a nomadic tribe that roamed the Rocky Mountains for generations. Exploring the Ute Trail becomes a journey through time, allowing you to connect with the cultural heritage of Aspen and gain a deeper understanding of the symbiotic relationship between the land and its first inhabitants.

Wildlife Encounters Along the Ute Trail

Aspen's wilderness comes alive along the Ute Trail, offering glimpses of its diverse wildlife. Keep a watchful eye for mule deer gracefully navigating the terrain and elusive foxes darting through the underbrush. Birdwatchers will delight in spotting various avian species, from the majestic golden eagle to the melodious songbirds that inhabit the alpine meadows.

For a truly enchanting experience, time your hike to coincide with the dawn or dusk hours when wildlife activity peaks. The Ute Trail provides a front-row seat to nature's theater, where each turn in the trail may reveal a new and fascinating encounter with the local fauna.

Hiking Tips and Considerations

While the Ute Trail is accessible to hikers of various skill levels, proper preparation ensures a safe and enjoyable journey. Here are some essential tips and considerations for those venturing onto the Ute Trail:

- Trail Conditions: Check trail conditions before embarking on your hike. Weather in the mountains can be unpredictable, and conditions may vary based on the season.
- Footwear: Wear sturdy and comfortable hiking boots with good traction to navigate the diverse terrain of the trail.
- Hydration: Bring an ample supply of water, especially during the warmer months. Staying hydrated is crucial for an enjoyable and safe hiking experience.
- Sun Protection: As you ascend to higher elevations, the sun's intensity increases. Apply sunscreen, wear a hat, and bring sunglasses to protect yourself from the sun's rays.
- Wildlife Etiquette: Respect the wildlife and maintain a safe distance. Keep a watchful eye on pets if you bring them along, as encounters with local fauna are not uncommon.
- Leave No Trace: Practice responsible hiking by leaving no trace of your visit. Pack out all trash and follow the principles of Leave No Trace to preserve the trail's pristine beauty.

Seasonal Considerations

The Ute Trail offers a different spectacle with each changing season, providing visitors with a reason to return year-round. Here's a glimpse of what each season brings to the Ute Trail:

- Spring: Witness the awakening of nature as wildflowers bloom, and the landscape transforms into a vibrant tapestry of colors. The air is crisp, and the scent of new growth fills the mountain air.

- Summer: Enjoy the warmth of the sun as you traverse the trail. The meadows come alive with activity, and the panoramic views are accentuated by clear skies. Summer offers ideal conditions for both novice and experienced hikers.
- Fall: As autumn paints the landscape with hues of gold and red, the Ute Trail becomes a mesmerizing journey through a sea of quaking aspen leaves. The crisp mountain air and the sound of leaves crunching beneath your feet create a quintessential fall experience.
- Winter: For those seeking a winter adventure, the Ute Trail transforms into a snow-covered wonderland. Snowshoeing and cross-country skiing become popular activities, allowing visitors to experience the serene beauty of Aspen's winter landscape.

3.16 Snowmass Village

In this comprehensive exploration, we unveil the must-visit points of interest in Snowmass Village, ensuring that every tourist's journey is filled with unforgettable experiences.

1. Skiing and Snowboarding Extravaganza at Snowmass Ski Area:

Snowmass Ski Area, a jewel in the crown of Aspen's winter offerings, beckons winter sports enthusiasts with an unparalleled extravaganza. As one of the largest and most renowned ski resorts in the United States, it's not merely a destination; it's a winter wonderland where adrenaline and awe coalesce. The resort sprawls across a vast expanse, boasting an extensive network of trails that cater to individuals of all skill levels, from novices seeking gentle slopes to seasoned experts craving challenging terrain.

The winter season transforms Snowmass into a pristine playground, where the crisp mountain air and fresh powder conspire to create an idyllic setting for winter sports. Skiers and snowboarders alike find themselves immersed in a world of possibilities, whether carving through immaculate corduroy on groomed runs or tackling the thrilling bumps and glades that characterize the more advanced areas of the resort.

The meticulously groomed slopes ensure a smooth and enjoyable experience for those just starting their snow sports journey. Beginners can confidently take their first turns under the guidance of expert instructors, while children can revel in the magic of snow-filled adventures at the dedicated learning areas.

For the seasoned thrill-seekers, Snowmass doesn't disappoint. The resort's diverse terrain includes challenging black diamond runs, thrilling moguls, and expansive bowls that provide an adrenaline rush against the backdrop of stunning alpine scenery. Freestyle enthusiasts can showcase their skills in the terrain parks, featuring jumps, rails, and other features designed to ignite creativity and progression.

Beyond the slopes, Snowmass Ski Area offers a host of amenities to enhance the overall experience. Modern and comfortable lodges provide respite from the cold, where skiers can enjoy delicious meals and hot beverages while soaking in the mountain views. The vibrant apres-ski scene adds a social dimension, with lively bars and restaurants creating an atmosphere of camaraderie and celebration.

2. Hiking and Biking Adventures on Snowmass Mountain:

As the winter snow gracefully bows out, Snowmass Mountain undergoes a transformative shift, becoming a haven for hikers and mountain bikers seeking to explore its breathtaking terrain. A vast network of trails, varying in difficulty, crisscrosses the landscape, inviting visitors to embark on adventures ranging from scenic strolls to heart-pounding ascents.

The postcard-worthy views from Snowmass Mountain are nothing short of breathtaking. Panoramas of the Elk Mountain Range and the Roaring Fork Valley stretch as far as the eye can see, rewarding hikers with a sense of accomplishment and a profound connection to the surrounding natural beauty. The summer season opens up a different dimension of exploration, where vibrant wildflowers carpet the meadows, and wildlife occasionally graces the trails.

For hikers, a variety of trails cater to different preferences and fitness levels. Casual strollers may opt for leisurely paths, such as the Nature Trail, offering informative signage about the local flora and fauna. More adventurous hikers can tackle challenging routes like the Rim Trail, which traces the mountain's perimeter and offers awe-inspiring views throughout the journey.

Mountain bikers, too, find a playground of possibilities on Snowmass Mountain. Trails like the Tom Blake Trail and the

Government Trail provide thrilling descents through aspen groves and evergreen forests. The mountain's lift-served biking options make it accessible for riders of varying skill levels, ensuring that everyone can experience the joy of descending through alpine landscapes without the strenuous uphill climb.

The summer allure of Snowmass Mountain extends beyond physical activities, with guided tours, photography opportunities, and the chance to simply soak in the serenity of the mountains. It's a haven for those seeking both adventure and tranquility amid nature's grandeur.

3. Summer Events and Festivals:

While Snowmass Village may be synonymous with winter sports, the village comes alive in a different vibrancy during the summer months. The transformation is marked by a vibrant array of events and festivals that capture the spirit of the season, providing a kaleidoscope of entertainment for locals and visitors alike.

The centerpiece of summer in Snowmass is the Snowmass Free Concert Series, held on the picturesque Fanny Hill. This open-air venue welcomes renowned musicians, offering a diverse range of musical genres that resonates through the mountain air. The family-friendly atmosphere and lively performances make it a favorite gathering spot for both locals and tourists.

Art enthusiasts will find themselves immersed in the cultural tapestry of Snowmass during the summer. The village hosts outdoor art exhibitions, showcasing works by local and regional artists against the stunning backdrop of the mountains. The Snowmass Arts Advisory Board actively curates these displays, fostering a sense of community and celebrating the creative spirit.

Culinary delights take center stage during the summer festivals in Snowmass. Food and wine festivals highlight the diverse flavors of the region, bringing together local chefs, winemakers, and food enthusiasts for a gastronomic celebration. Visitors can indulge in tastings, attend cooking demonstrations, and savor the fusion of mountain-inspired cuisine.

Beyond the music, art, and culinary experiences, Snowmass embraces a range of summer activities, including yoga festivals, outdoor film nights, and adventure races. The village's charming streets become a canvas for street performers and artisans, creating a dynamic and engaging atmosphere for all who stroll through.

4. The Snowmass Ice Age Discovery Center: A Journey Through Time

Nestled within Snowmass Village, the Snowmass Ice Age Discovery Center stands as a time capsule, inviting visitors to delve into the prehistoric past. In 2010, the discovery of ancient mammoth remains and other Ice Age creatures unearthed a wealth of knowledge about the region's rich history. This fascinating museum offers more than just exhibits; it provides a hands-on and interactive experience for those curious about the ancient ecosystems that once thrived in the area.

As you step into the center, the atmosphere becomes a portal to a bygone era. Real fossils, meticulously preserved, line the exhibits, allowing visitors to touch and feel the remnants of creatures that roamed the Snowmass region thousands of years ago. The museum's knowledgeable staff adds a layer of depth to the experience, offering insights into the science and discovery behind each exhibit.

One of the center's highlights is the mammoth excavation site replica. This carefully recreated scene takes you back to the moment when paleontologists made the groundbreaking discovery. The detailed exhibits provide a vivid narrative of the Ice Age, showcasing the flora and fauna that characterized this ancient landscape. From towering mastodons to ancient plant species, the Snowmass Ice Age Discovery Center paints a comprehensive picture of the region's geological and biological evolution.

For those with a thirst for knowledge, the center hosts educational programs and workshops, making it an ideal destination for families and school groups. Visitors of all ages can participate in fossil casting or engage in interactive displays that simulate the excavation process. It's a rare opportunity to become an amateur paleontologist, uncovering the mysteries of the past.

5. Base Village: A Culinary and Retail Haven

After a day of exploration and discovery, Base Village emerges as the perfect place to unwind, indulge, and immerse yourself in the vibrant heart of Snowmass. This lively hub offers a diverse array of dining, shopping, and entertainment options, ensuring that every taste and preference is catered to.

For culinary enthusiasts, Base Village is a paradise. A myriad of restaurants, cafes, and pubs line the charming streets, serving up a delightful mix of local and international cuisine. From upscale dining establishments with panoramic mountain views to cozy cafes offering comforting bites, Base Village satisfies every palate. Whether you're in the mood for a hearty après-ski meal, a leisurely brunch, or an evening of fine dining, the village has a culinary experience waiting for you.

The boutiques and shops of Base Village add another layer to the experience. Charming storefronts beckon with unique treasures, from locally crafted souvenirs to high-end fashion and outdoor gear. Stroll through the village, and you'll find a blend of curated boutiques, outdoor adventure stores, and art galleries. It's the perfect place for a leisurely shopping spree, allowing you to take a piece of Snowmass home with you.

As the sun sets, Base Village transforms into a hub of entertainment. Live music performances, cultural events, and festivals often grace the village square, creating an atmosphere that resonates with the vibrancy of Snowmass. It's a place where locals and visitors converge, sharing stories, laughter, and the joy of being surrounded by the beauty of the mountains.

6. Snowmass Golf Course: Where Scenic Tee Time Meets Mountain Majesty

For those seeking a different kind of adventure amidst the stunning landscapes of Snowmass, the Snowmass Golf Course offers a serene escape. Set against the backdrop of mountainous terrain, this golf course provides not only a challenging round for enthusiasts but also a picturesque experience for all.

The course design takes full advantage of the natural beauty surrounding it. Lush fairways weave through meadows and pockets of aspen groves, providing a tranquil and scenic environment for golfers. With the snow-capped peaks as a backdrop, every swing becomes a moment to savor the majesty of the mountains.

Whether you're an experienced golfer looking for a challenging game or a beginner seeking a leisurely round, the Snowmass Golf Course accommodates all skill levels. The well-manicured fairways and greens ensure that every shot is played against a stunning canvas of mountain vistas, creating an idyllic setting for a day on the links.

7. Snowmass Rodeo: Cowboy Culture in the Mountains:

Embracing the spirit of the Wild West, the Snowmass Rodeo stands as a summertime tradition that seamlessly brings cowboy culture to the heart of the mountains. As the sun sets over the rugged peaks, visitors gather to witness thrilling rodeo events that transport them back in time. The arena comes alive with the pulse-pounding excitement of bull riding, where daring riders attempt to conquer the mighty beasts, showcasing the epitome of cowboy courage. Barrel racing adds a touch of finesse to the rodeo, as skilled riders navigate a series of tight turns around barrels at breakneck speeds.

Beyond the exhilarating rodeo events, the Snowmass Rodeo offers a delightful array of entertainment for the entire family. Live music sets the backdrop, infusing the mountain air with the soulful tunes of country melodies. The aroma of delicious barbecue wafts through the venue, tempting visitors with the sizzle of grills and the promise of a satisfying Western feast. Families can indulge in mouthwatering treats, from smoked meats to classic sides, creating a true cowboy culinary experience.

Family-friendly activities abound, making the Snowmass Rodeo a wholesome outing for all ages. Children can partake in pony rides, face painting, and interactive games, creating lasting memories against the backdrop of the majestic mountains. The sense of community and camaraderie during the Snowmass Rodeo echoes the close-knit spirit of the Old West, where neighbors gathered for shared experiences and celebrations.

The beauty of the Snowmass Rodeo lies not only in its thrilling events but also in its ability to transport visitors into a bygone era. Against the backdrop of the mountain setting, the rodeo captures the essence of the Old West, creating a timeless atmosphere where tradition meets contemporary revelry.

8. Balloon Rides Over Snowmass: A Sky-High Adventure:

For those seeking a sky-high adventure and a unique perspective of Snowmass, the option of embarking on a hot air balloon ride presents itself as an extraordinary opportunity. Ascending high above the village and the surrounding mountain landscapes, participants find themselves in the serene vantage point of a balloon basket. The experience unfolds as a visual feast, providing a bird's-eye view of the majestic peaks, sprawling valleys, and the charming village nestled below.

As the balloon gently glides through the crisp mountain air, passengers are treated to panoramic vistas that stretch as far as the eye can see. The tranquil flight over Snowmass allows for a peaceful immersion in the breathtaking scenery, creating a sense of awe and wonder. The natural beauty of the mountains, enhanced by the soft hues of dawn or the warm glow of sunset, becomes an intimate and unparalleled spectacle.

Balloon rides over Snowmass offer a unique blend of tranquility and adventure, appealing to those who seek a slower-paced exploration of the stunning landscapes. The experience provides ample opportunities for photography enthusiasts to capture the ever-changing play of light on the mountainous terrain. Whether soaring above dense forests, meandering rivers, or the charming village below, each moment in the balloon becomes a timeless encounter with the natural wonders of Snowmass.

9. Snowmass Village Recreation Center: Indoor Fun for All Ages:

While Snowmass is renowned for its outdoor adventures, the Snowmass Village Recreation Center ensures that the fun doesn't have to pause, even on a snowy day. This indoor haven caters to visitors of all ages, offering a diverse array of activities that promise entertainment and relaxation.

Swimming in the pool becomes a delightful escape, where families can enjoy a refreshing dip or engage in playful water activities. For those seeking the thrill of gliding on ice, the recreation center features an ice-skating rink, providing a classic winter experience. The sound of skates gliding over the ice resonates through the facility, creating an atmosphere of wintertime joy.

Basketball enthusiasts can indulge in friendly games on the indoor courts, and fitness enthusiasts will find a well-equipped gym to maintain their workout routines. The Snowmass Village Recreation Center embodies versatility, ensuring that every member of the family can find an activity to suit their preferences, making it a perfect retreat on days when the weather calls for indoor adventures.

10. Local Art and Culture: The Collective Snowmass:

Immersing oneself in the vibrant art and culture scene of Snowmass Village unfolds as a captivating experience at The Collective Snowmass. This community-driven space serves as a dynamic hub for creativity, hosting an eclectic array of events that showcase the talent and diversity of the local arts community.

Art enthusiasts can explore ever-changing exhibitions, featuring works by local and regional artists. From paintings and sculptures to multimedia installations, The Collective Snowmass offers a visual journey that captures the essence of the mountain community. The space encourages dialogue and appreciation for artistic expression, creating an environment where creativity flourishes.

Beyond visual arts, The Collective Snowmass serves as a venue for live performances, including music, theater, and dance. The stage comes alive with the energy of performers, bringing a cultural vibrancy to the heart of the village.

Visitors can enjoy a range of events, from intimate acoustic sessions to lively community celebrations.

Workshops and community gatherings further enhance the interactive nature of The Collective Snowmass. Whether participating in a hands-on art class or attending a thought-provoking discussion, visitors can actively engage with the local community and contribute to the cultural tapestry of Snowmass Village.

CHAPTER FOUR

NAVIGATING ASPEN

4.1 Transportation Options

Aspen, nestled in the heart of the Rocky Mountains, offers a variety of transportation options to cater to the diverse needs of tourists. Whether you're arriving at the Aspen/Pitkin County Airport or exploring the town and its surrounding areas, here's a guide to the transportation choices available.

4.1.1 Aspen/Pitkin County Airport (ASE):

For travelers embarking on a journey to Aspen, the Aspen/Pitkin County Airport (ASE) serves as the primary gateway to this picturesque destination. Situated just a few miles from downtown Aspen, ASE is a well-equipped and convenient airport catering to both domestic and seasonal international flights. Here's a comprehensive guide to help tourists navigate Aspen's airport seamlessly.

1. Arriving at Aspen/Pitkin County Airport:

Upon landing at ASE, visitors are greeted with the breathtaking backdrop of the Rocky Mountains. The airport's compact size ensures a hassle-free experience, with a straightforward layout that facilitates easy navigation. Baggage claim, rental car services, and ground transportation options are conveniently located, allowing for a swift transition from the runway to your desired destination in Aspen.

2. Ground Transportation Options:

Taxi Services: Taxis are readily available at the airport, providing a convenient and quick means of transportation to various accommodations in Aspen. The journey from the airport to downtown is relatively short, allowing you to start your Aspen adventure promptly.

Shuttle Services: Numerous shuttle services operate at ASE, offering shared and private rides to different parts of Aspen. These services are not only cost-effective but also provide an opportunity to enjoy the scenic drive to your destination.

Rental Cars: For those seeking flexibility in exploring Aspen and its surroundings, rental car services are available at the airport. A variety of car rental agencies have offices on-site, allowing tourists to choose the vehicle that suits their preferences and travel plans.

3. Facilities and Services:

Airport Amenities: Despite its size, ASE offers a range of amenities to ensure passenger comfort. These include dining options, souvenir shops, and services like baggage assistance. The airport's cozy atmosphere provides a welcoming introduction to Aspen.

Wi-Fi and Connectivity: Stay connected during your time at ASE with complimentary Wi-Fi services. This enables travelers to check flight information, communicate with loved ones, or make last-minute plans for their Aspen stay.

Visitor Information: ASE is equipped with information counters and friendly staff ready to assist tourists with any inquiries. Whether you need maps, local event details, or transportation advice, the airport's personnel are dedicated to ensuring a smooth start to your Aspen visit.

4. Seasonal Considerations:

Winter Preparations: During the winter months, it's essential to be mindful of weather conditions. Snowfall and icy roads can impact travel plans, so staying informed about weather updates and being prepared for winter driving conditions is advisable.

Summer Enjoyment: In the summer, the airport's surroundings come alive with lush greenery and clear skies. Take advantage of the pleasant weather and explore the outdoor activities that Aspen has to offer.

5. Aspen/Pitkin County Airport Expansion:

As a testament to Aspen's growing popularity as a travel destination, there have been ongoing efforts to enhance ASE's facilities. Travelers can expect improvements in infrastructure, additional services, and increased capacity to accommodate the rising number of visitors to this mountain resort town.

4.1.2 Shuttle Services:

This section provides essential information on Aspen's shuttle services, offering insights into their features, benefits, and how to make the most of this convenient transportation choice.

Key Features of Shuttle Services:

- Accessibility: Shuttle services in Aspen operate on a well-organized and accessible network, making them an ideal choice for tourists. The services connect major points of interest, including the Aspen/Pitkin County Airport, hotels, ski resorts, and popular landmarks, ensuring you can easily reach your desired destinations.

- Shared and Private Options: Aspen's shuttle services cater to various preferences, offering both shared and private transportation options. Shared shuttles are a cost-effective choice for budget-conscious travelers, while private shuttles provide exclusivity and flexibility for those seeking a more personalized experience.

- Scheduled Routes: The shuttle services in Aspen follow scheduled routes, providing a reliable timetable for pickups and drop-offs. This predictability allows you to plan your journeys efficiently, whether you're heading to the slopes for a day of skiing or exploring the vibrant downtown area.

- Hotel Connections: Many shuttle services have designated stops at popular hotels, ensuring convenient and door-to-door transportation. Upon arriving at the Aspen/Pitkin County Airport, check with your accommodation to inquire about shuttle services that may have direct routes to your hotel.

- Luggage Handling: Shuttle services in Aspen are designed to accommodate the needs of travelers, including luggage handling. Professional drivers assist with loading and unloading luggage, making your journey hassle-free and allowing you to focus on enjoying the scenic views and amenities Aspen has to offer.

Making the Most of Shuttle Services:

- Advance Reservations: To secure your spot on a shuttle and streamline your arrival process, consider making advance reservations. Many shuttle services allow online booking, enabling you to plan your transportation ahead of time and avoid potential delays.
- Knowledge of Routes: Familiarize yourself with the shuttle routes and stops in Aspen. This knowledge can be particularly beneficial when planning your daily activities, ensuring you choose the most convenient shuttle for your intended destinations.
- Flexible Schedules: While shuttle services adhere to set schedules, it's essential to consider their frequency and operational hours. Some services may have more flexible schedules during peak seasons, catering to the increased influx of tourists.
- Group Travel: If you're traveling with a group, inquire about group rates and private shuttle options. Group discounts and private shuttles provide a cost-effective and efficient means of transportation, especially when accommodating multiple travelers with varied itineraries.
- Local Insights: Don't hesitate to seek advice from locals or your accommodation's concierge regarding the best shuttle services for your specific needs. Locals

often have valuable insights into the most efficient routes and reliable shuttle companies.

4.1.3 Rental Cars:

Here's everything you need to know about renting a car in Aspen, allowing you to navigate the surrounding areas at your own pace.

- Convenient Airport Access: Upon arrival at the Aspen/Pitkin County Airport (ASE), you'll find several reputable car rental agencies conveniently located at the airport. This allows for a seamless transition from your flight to the driver's seat, ready to embark on your Aspen adventure.
- Consider Seasonal Conditions: Aspen experiences distinct seasons, each offering unique attractions. If you plan to visit during the winter months for the world-renowned skiing, ensure your rental car is equipped for snowy and icy conditions. Most rental agencies in Aspen provide vehicles with snow tires and other winter-ready features.
- Booking in Advance: To secure the vehicle that best suits your needs, it's advisable to book your rental car in advance. This becomes especially important during peak seasons when demand is high. Reserving early ensures a broader selection of vehicles and often better rates.
- Choosing the Right Vehicle: Aspen's mountainous terrain may influence your choice of rental vehicle. If you plan to explore off-the-beaten-path destinations or engage in outdoor activities, consider renting an

SUV or a vehicle with four-wheel drive for better traction on mountain roads.

- Understanding Rental Policies: Before confirming your reservation, carefully review the rental policies of the chosen agency. Take note of fuel policies, mileage limits, and any additional fees that may apply. Understanding the terms will help you avoid surprises and ensure a smooth rental experience.

- Exploring Beyond Aspen: While the town itself is charming and full of attractions, having a rental car provides the opportunity to explore the scenic surroundings. Drive to the Maroon Bells, take a road trip along Independence Pass, or visit nearby towns like Snowmass for a broader Rocky Mountain experience.

- Parking in Aspen: Parking is generally available in Aspen, but it's essential to be aware of parking regulations. Some hotels offer complimentary parking, while others may charge a fee. In the town center, you'll find metered parking and public lots, making it convenient to explore Aspen on foot after parking your car.

- Fueling Up: Ensure you're familiar with the location of gas stations in Aspen, especially if you plan to venture into the surrounding areas. While Aspen itself has gas stations, more remote locations may have limited options.

- Returning the Rental Car: When it's time to depart, return your rental car to the designated location. Most rental agencies have drop-off points at the airport, making it convenient for those catching outgoing flights. Be sure to return the vehicle on time to avoid any additional charges.

4.1.4 Local Buses:

Navigating the town and its surroundings is made easy with the comprehensive network of local buses operated by the Roaring Fork Transportation Authority (RFTA). Whether you're a budget-conscious traveler or someone looking to reduce their environmental footprint, the local buses in Aspen provide a convenient and reliable way to explore the area.

Understanding the RFTA Bus System:

The Roaring Fork Transportation Authority operates an extensive bus network that covers Aspen, Snowmass Village, and nearby communities. The RFTA buses are easily identifiable with their distinctive blue and black color scheme. Understanding the key components of the RFTA bus system will help you make the most of this mode of transportation:

- Routes and Schedules: RFTA offers a variety of routes catering to different destinations within Aspen and the surrounding areas. The routes are well-marked, and each bus stop provides information on the specific route, schedule, and destinations served. It's advisable to pick up a printed schedule or access the online schedule to plan your journey in advance.
- Fare System: RFTA has a fare system based on the distance traveled. Be sure to have the correct fare ready when boarding the bus. Exact change is appreciated, or you can use the convenient RFTA app,

which allows you to purchase and store digital tickets on your smartphone.

- Bike-Friendly Buses: Aspen is a bike-friendly town, and RFTA buses are equipped with bike racks. If you're planning to explore the town on two wheels, simply load and unload your bike at designated stops. This feature adds an extra layer of flexibility to your transportation options.
- Frequency of Service: The frequency of bus service varies depending on the route and the time of day. Popular routes, such as those connecting downtown Aspen and Snowmass Village, generally have more frequent service, especially during peak hours.

4.2 Travel Safety Tips

Ensuring your safety while exploring Aspen is paramount. Whether you're engaging in outdoor adventures or immersing yourself in the town's cultural offerings, following these travel safety tips will contribute to a secure and enjoyable experience.

1. Weather Awareness: Aspen's mountainous terrain means weather conditions can change rapidly. Stay informed about the forecast, especially during winter, and be prepared for sudden changes in temperature and precipitation. Dress in layers and carry essentials like water, snacks, and a map.

2. Altitude Adjustment: Aspen sits at a high altitude, and visitors may experience symptoms of altitude sickness. Stay hydrated, avoid excessive alcohol consumption during the first few days, and allow your body time to acclimate to the altitude.

3. Outdoor Adventure Caution: If you're partaking in outdoor activities such as hiking or skiing, adhere to safety guidelines. Inform someone about your plans, carry necessary gear, and be aware of trail difficulty levels. Check for trail closures or warnings before embarking on your adventure.

4. Wildlife Interaction: Aspen's natural beauty includes a diverse range of wildlife. Respect their habitats and maintain a safe distance. Do not feed or approach wild animals, and store food securely to prevent attracting them to your accommodation.

5. Secure Your Belongings: While Aspen is a relatively safe destination, it's essential to practice common-sense precautions. Keep valuables secure, be cautious in crowded areas, and use hotel safes for important documents and items.

4.3 Tips for Navigating Public Transportation

1. Familiarize Yourself with the Routes:

Study the route maps provided by the Roaring Fork Transportation Authority (RFTA). Understanding the bus routes and schedules is crucial for planning your journey effectively. Identify the key stops and the destinations they serve to make informed decisions about your travel routes.

2. Plan Ahead:

Check the bus schedules in advance and plan your trips accordingly. Buses in Aspen operate on a fixed schedule, so arriving a few minutes early at the designated stops ensures you won't miss your ride. Consider using mobile apps or online resources that provide real-time information on bus locations and arrival times.

3. Purchase Multi-Day Passes:

If you plan to use public transportation frequently during your stay, consider purchasing multi-day passes. These passes offer cost savings compared to individual fares and provide flexibility for unlimited rides within the specified duration. They can be convenient for tourists exploring Aspen over an extended period.

4. Be Early and Patient:

Arriving a little earlier at the bus stops ensures you have enough time to board, especially during peak hours. Public transportation in Aspen is generally reliable, but factors like weather conditions or heavy traffic can affect schedules. Exercise patience, and if your schedule allows, opt for less busy travel times.

5. Ask for Assistance:

Don't hesitate to ask for assistance if you're unsure about which bus to take or need guidance on routes. Locals and transportation staff are typically friendly and willing to help. Bus drivers, in particular, can provide valuable information about routes, stops, and any changes in the schedule.

6. Utilize Connectivity:

Aspen's public transportation system is well-connected, providing easy access to popular destinations, including ski resorts, cultural attractions, and shopping districts. Take advantage of the comprehensive network to explore various facets of Aspen without the hassle of navigating through traffic or finding parking.

7. Know the Fare System:

Familiarize yourself with the fare system, including the cost of single rides and any discounts available. Exact change is appreciated when paying in cash. If you plan to use public transportation frequently, explore the various pass options for added convenience and savings.

8. Be Mindful of Peak Hours:

Consider the peak hours for public transportation, especially during the morning and evening rush. If your schedule permits, try to travel during off-peak hours to avoid crowded buses and potential delays. This can contribute to a more comfortable and relaxed commuting experience.

9. Respect Local Etiquette:

Practice good public transportation etiquette. Yield seats to those in need, keep noise levels to a minimum, and follow any guidelines or rules posted inside the buses. Being considerate of fellow passengers contributes to a positive and harmonious travel experience for everyone.

10. Explore Alternative Modes of Transportation:

While buses are the primary mode of public transportation, consider exploring alternative options like walking or biking for shorter distances within Aspen. Many areas of interest are pedestrian-friendly, allowing you to enjoy the town's charm at a leisurely pace.

4.4 Travel Insurance and its Importance

One crucial aspect of travel planning that often goes overlooked is obtaining comprehensive travel insurance. In this guide, we'll explore the importance of travel insurance for tourists visiting Aspen and highlight the key factors to consider when selecting the right coverage.

Why is Travel Insurance Important?

1. Financial Protection:

Unforeseen events can disrupt travel plans, leading to financial losses. Travel insurance acts as a safety net, providing coverage for non-refundable expenses such as airfare, accommodations, and pre-booked activities in case your trip is canceled or interrupted due to unexpected circumstances.

2. Medical Emergencies:

Aspen's high-altitude environment and the allure of outdoor activities increase the risk of accidents or health issues. Travel insurance with emergency medical coverage ensures you receive prompt and necessary medical attention without the burden of exorbitant expenses.

3. Trip Delay and Missed Connections:

Weather conditions, particularly during winter, can result in travel delays. Travel insurance can reimburse additional expenses incurred due to delays, such as accommodation and meals. It also provides assistance in the event of missed connections.

4. Baggage and Personal Belongings Protection:

Losing luggage or having personal belongings stolen can be a significant inconvenience. Travel insurance offers coverage for lost, stolen, or damaged luggage, providing reimbursement for the value of your belongings.

5. Adventure Sports Coverage:

Aspen is renowned for its outdoor adventures, including skiing, snowboarding, and mountain biking. Ensure your travel insurance covers these specific activities to protect against injuries or accidents related to adventurous pursuits.

6. Emergency Evacuation and Repatriation:

In the rare event of a medical emergency requiring evacuation to a medical facility or repatriation to your home country, travel insurance ensures that necessary arrangements are made without imposing exorbitant costs on you.

7. Peace of Mind:

Knowing that you are covered in the face of unexpected events provides peace of mind, allowing you to fully enjoy your time in Aspen. Whether you're exploring the scenic trails, indulging in winter sports, or immersing yourself in the town's cultural offerings, travel insurance enhances your overall travel experience.

Types of Coverage to Consider:

1. Trip Cancellation and Interruption:

Protects your investment by reimbursing non-refundable expenses if your trip is canceled or interrupted due to covered reasons such as illness, injury, or family emergencies.

2. Emergency Medical and Dental Coverage:

Covers medical and dental expenses incurred during your trip, ensuring you receive necessary healthcare without financial strain.

3. Travel Delay and Missed Connections:

Reimburses additional expenses caused by travel delays and offers assistance in case of missed connections.

4. Baggage and Personal Belongings:

Provides coverage for lost, stolen, or damaged luggage, allowing you to replace essential items during your trip.

5. Adventure Sports Coverage:

Specifically tailored for activities like skiing, snowboarding, and mountain biking, offering protection against injuries or accidents related to these pursuits.

6. Emergency Evacuation and Repatriation:

Ensures that you receive prompt and secure evacuation or repatriation in case of a medical emergency.

7. 24/7 Assistance Services:

Access to professional help and guidance, offering support in medical emergencies, travel advice, and overall assistance throughout your journey.

CHAPTER FIVE

ACCOMMODATION

5.1 Hotels and Resorts

Aspen, nestled in the heart of the Colorado Rockies, offers a diverse range of accommodation options to suit every traveler's preferences. From luxurious hotels and resorts to boutique stays and budget-friendly options, the city caters to a spectrum of tastes and budgets.

For those seeking the pinnacle of luxury, Aspen boasts renowned hotels and resorts that redefine opulence. The St. Regis Aspen Resort, with its world-class amenities and personalized service, stands as an epitome of sophistication. From lavish suites to exquisite dining experiences, guests are immersed in a realm of indulgence. Another gem is The Little Nell, an iconic hotel at the base of Aspen Mountain, offering unparalleled access to both winter and summer adventures. With impeccable service and stunning mountain views, it epitomizes mountain luxury.

Recommended Hotels And Resorts With Their Locations

1. The St. Regis Aspen Resort

Location: 315 East Dean Street, Aspen, CO 81611, USA

Description: Situated at the base of Aspen Mountain, The St. Regis Aspen Resort is an iconic luxury destination. With its convenient downtown location, guests have easy access to Aspen's renowned shopping, dining, and cultural attractions.

The resort offers opulent accommodations, world-class dining, and a spa, providing an unparalleled mountain retreat.

2. The Little Nell

Location: 675 East Durant Avenue, Aspen, CO 81611, USA

Description: Nestled at the foot of Aspen Mountain, The Little Nell is a five-star hotel renowned for its exclusivity and exceptional service. Its central location allows guests to ski in and out during winter and explore downtown Aspen in summer. The hotel features elegantly appointed rooms, gourmet dining, and personalized concierge services.

3. Limelight Hotel Aspen

Location: 355 South Monarch Street, Aspen, CO 81611, USA

Description: The Limelight Hotel is located in the heart of Aspen, offering a contemporary and lively atmosphere. With proximity to Aspen Mountain and downtown, guests enjoy easy access to both outdoor activities and cultural attractions. The hotel emphasizes comfort, providing modern rooms, an outdoor pool, and an inviting lounge area.

4. Hotel Jerome, Auberge Resorts Collection

Location: 330 East Main Street, Aspen, CO 81611, USA

Description: A historic landmark, Hotel Jerome combines Victorian charm with luxurious amenities. Situated in downtown Aspen, the hotel is close to Aspen's vibrant nightlife, art galleries, and outdoor adventures. Guests can savor the timeless elegance of this Auberge Resorts

Collection property while enjoying top-notch service and sophisticated accommodations.

5. The Gant

Location: 610 South West End Street, Aspen, CO 81611, USA

Description: For those seeking a unique accommodation experience, The Gant offers privately owned condominiums surrounded by Aspen's natural beauty. Located a short walk from downtown, this property provides a peaceful retreat with fully equipped kitchens, spacious living areas, and easy access to hiking trails and ski slopes.

5.2 Boutique Stays

If your preference leans towards unique and intimate experiences, Aspen's boutique stays are sure to captivate you. The Limelight Hotel, with its contemporary design and vibrant atmosphere, provides a chic and cozy retreat. This boutique gem is centrally located, making it convenient for exploring Aspen's attractions. For a blend of history and charm, The Jerome Hotel is an excellent choice. With its Victorian architecture and modern amenities, it offers a boutique experience infused with Aspen's rich heritage.

Recommended Boutique Stays With Their Locations

1. Annabelle Inn

Location: 232 West Main Street, Aspen, CO 81611, USA

Description: Tucked away on West Main Street, the Annabelle Inn is a charming boutique stay with a European-inspired ambiance. Each room is uniquely decorated, creating a cozy and intimate atmosphere. The inn's location offers a serene retreat while keeping guests close to Aspen's downtown attractions and outdoor activities.

2. Molly Gibson Lodge

Location: 101 West Main Street, Aspen, CO 81611, USA

Description: The Molly Gibson Lodge is a boutique stay that combines affordability with a welcoming atmosphere. Located on West Main Street, this lodge offers comfortable accommodations and a range of amenities. Guests can easily access downtown Aspen and nearby outdoor attractions, making it a convenient choice for budget-conscious travelers.

3. Hotel Aspen

Location: 110 West Main Street, Aspen, CO 81611, USA

Description: Hotel Aspen, situated on West Main Street, is a boutique retreat that captures the spirit of Aspen's mountain charm. With its intimate setting and personalized service, guests experience a cozy escape while being just steps away from downtown shops, restaurants, and cultural hotspots. The hotel's warm ambiance and mountain-inspired decor make it a delightful boutique stay in the heart of Aspen.

5.3 Budget-Friendly Options

Aspen recognizes the value of budget-conscious travelers and provides accommodation options that balance affordability with comfort. The Mountain Chalet Aspen is a prime example, offering reasonable rates without compromising on quality. Its central location and cozy ambiance make it an excellent choice for those looking to explore Aspen on a budget. Additionally, the Molly Gibson Lodge provides affordable accommodations without sacrificing proximity to Aspen's downtown and outdoor activities.

Recommended Budget-Friendly Accommodation With Their Locations

1. Mountain Chalet Aspen

Location: 333 East Durant Avenue, Aspen, CO 81611, USA

Description: The Mountain Chalet Aspen is a budget-friendly accommodation option located conveniently near downtown Aspen. Offering a cozy atmosphere and basic amenities, it provides a comfortable stay without breaking the bank. Its central location allows guests easy access to Aspen's attractions, making it an excellent choice for budget-conscious travelers.

2. Aspen Mountain Lodge

Location: 311 West Main Street, Aspen, CO 81611, USA

Description: The Aspen Mountain Lodge, located on West Main Street, caters to budget-conscious travelers seeking simplicity and value. With comfortable rooms and a convenient location, this lodge allows guests to enjoy Aspen's downtown area and outdoor attractions without straining their wallets.

3. St. Moritz Lodge & Condominiums

Location: 334 West Hyman Avenue, Aspen, CO 81611, USA

Description: The St. Moritz Lodge & Condominiums offers affordable lodging options on West Hyman Avenue. With a range of room types and shared facilities, this budget-friendly accommodation provides a practical and comfortable stay. Guests can easily access Aspen's downtown scene and outdoor recreational opportunities.

4. Aspenalt Lodge

Location: 157 Basalt Center Circle, Basalt, CO 81621, USA

Description: The Aspenalt Lodge, located in nearby Basalt, provides a cost-effective alternative for those willing to explore the outskirts of Aspen. This lodge offers a serene atmosphere and basic amenities while allowing guests to enjoy a budget-friendly stay. The location provides easy access to both Aspen and the surrounding natural beauty.

5.4 Unique Accommodation Experiences

For travelers seeking a touch of uniqueness in their stay, Aspen delivers with a range of distinctive accommodation experiences. The historic Hotel Jerome, originally built in the late 19th century, blends classic elegance with modern amenities. Its storied past and architectural charm create an unforgettable atmosphere. For a more unconventional stay, consider The Gant, a collection of privately owned condominiums. This offers a home-away-from-home experience, complete with fully equipped kitchens and spacious living areas, perfect for extended stays or families.

Recommended Unique Accommodation With Their Locations

1. Aspen Meadows Resort

Location: 845 Meadows Road, Aspen, CO 81611, USA

Description: Aspen Meadows Resort offers a unique stay with its Bauhaus-inspired architecture and stunning mountain views. Designed by Herbert Bayer, a prominent architect and artist, the resort provides a distinct ambiance. Located near the Aspen Institute, guests can immerse themselves in a cultural and artistic atmosphere while enjoying the resort's modern amenities.

2. Viceroy Snowmass

Location: 130 Wood Road, Snowmass Village, CO 81615, USA

Description: While not directly in Aspen, the Viceroy Snowmass offers a unique accommodation experience just a short drive away. This stylish resort is known for its modern design and ski-in/ski-out access. Guests can enjoy luxurious residences, a spa, and a rooftop pool with panoramic views, providing a unique and sophisticated mountain retreat.

5.5 Booking Accommodation in Advance

Whether you're visiting during the snow-covered winter months or the vibrant summer season, securing your lodging ahead of time offers several advantages and enhances your overall travel experience.

1. Ensures Availability:

Aspen is a highly sought-after destination throughout the year, attracting visitors with its world-class skiing, outdoor adventures, and cultural events. Booking your accommodation in advance guarantees that you have a wide range of options to choose from, allowing you to find the perfect lodging that suits your preferences, whether it's a cozy boutique stay, a luxurious resort, or a budget-friendly option.

2. Secures the Best Rates:

By booking in advance, you often have access to better rates and exclusive deals. Many hotels and resorts in Aspen offer early booking discounts or special packages that include added perks such as complimentary breakfast, spa credits, or discounted lift tickets. Securing your accommodation early not only ensures availability but also allows you to take advantage of cost-effective options.

3. Stress-Free Planning:

Planning your accommodation in advance contributes to a stress-free travel experience. Knowing that your lodging is confirmed allows you to focus on other aspects of your trip, such as crafting an itinerary, researching activities, and anticipating the unique offerings of Aspen. It provides peace of mind, especially during peak seasons when lodging availability can be limited.

4. Access to Special Packages:

Many accommodations in Aspen offer special packages that cater to specific interests or activities. These packages may include perks like guided outdoor excursions, spa treatments, or tickets to cultural events. Booking in advance enables you to explore these tailored packages and choose one that enhances your overall Aspen experience.

5. Flexibility with Room Preferences:

Booking accommodation in advance allows you to secure your preferred room type, whether it's a suite with a mountain view, a cozy room with a fireplace, or a family-friendly unit. Early reservations ensure that you have the flexibility to choose the accommodation that aligns with your specific needs and preferences.

6. Peace of Mind During Peak Seasons:

Aspen experiences peak seasons, particularly during winter for skiing enthusiasts and summer for outdoor adventurers. During these times, accommodation demand is high, and waiting until the last minute may result in limited choices and higher prices. Booking in advance provides the assurance that you have secured a comfortable place to stay, especially during peak tourist seasons.

7. Better Chance for Room Upgrades:

Hotels and resorts often appreciate guests who book in advance, and as a result, they may be more inclined to offer room upgrades or additional amenities. By demonstrating your commitment to your stay early on, you increase the likelihood of enjoying special perks that can elevate your overall lodging experience.

5.6 Tips for Finding the Right Lodging for Your Needs

1. Define Your Priorities:

Before starting your accommodation search, identify your priorities. Are you looking for proximity to ski slopes, downtown convenience, or a secluded mountain retreat? Knowing your preferences will help narrow down your options.

2. Set a Budget:

Establish a clear budget for accommodation, taking into account other expenses like dining, activities, and transportation. Aspen offers choices across a wide price range, ensuring there's something for every budget.

3. Research Amenities:

Consider the amenities that matter most to you. Whether it's a spa, on-site dining, pet-friendly options, or specific room features, understanding the available amenities will aid in selecting the perfect lodging.

4. Read Reviews:

Utilize online reviews from reputable platforms to gain insights into the experiences of previous guests. Pay attention to reviews that align with your priorities and expectations.

5. Flexible Dates:

If possible, maintain flexibility in your travel dates. This can open up more lodging options and may allow you to take advantage of lower rates during off-peak times.

6. Check for Special Packages:

Many hotels and resorts in Aspen offer special packages that include added perks like lift tickets, spa treatments, or dining credits. Explore these options to maximize the value of your stay.

7. Connect with Locals:

Engage with locals or travel communities to gather recommendations and insights. They can provide valuable tips on hidden gems or lesser-known accommodations that may align with your preferences.

CHAPTER SIX

DINING IN ASPEN

6.1 Must-Taste Dishes and Local Delicacies

1. Aspen Crud:

Description: Embark on a culinary journey through Aspen with the iconic Aspen Crud. This delightful concoction originated during the Prohibition era and combines vanilla ice cream, root beer, and a splash of bourbon. It's a sweet and boozy treat that captures the essence of Aspen's history and hospitality.

2. Elk Tenderloin:

Description: Immerse yourself in the flavors of the Rocky Mountains by indulging in Elk Tenderloin. This dish showcases the region's commitment to sustainable and locally sourced ingredients. The tender and succulent elk meat, often paired with mountain-inspired accompaniments, provides a true taste of Aspen's wilderness.

3. Truffle-Infused Macaroni and Cheese:

Description: Elevate your comfort food experience with Aspen's truffle-infused macaroni and cheese. The earthy and decadent aroma of truffles adds a touch of luxury to this classic dish. It's a must-try for those seeking a fusion of gourmet flavors in a cozy mountain setting.

4. Rocky Mountain Oysters:

Description: For the adventurous foodie, Rocky Mountain Oysters are a unique delicacy that reflects the rustic charm of Aspen. These crispy-fried bull testicles may sound unconventional, but they are a local favorite, offering a distinctive taste of the Wild West.

5. Miso-Glazed Black Cod:

Description: Explore the intersection of Asian and mountain flavors with Miso-Glazed Black Cod. This dish combines the delicate and buttery texture of black cod with the umami richness of miso glaze. It's a perfect representation of Aspen's diverse culinary influences.

6. Truffle Fries:

Description: Indulge in the simple yet irresistible pleasure of truffle fries. Aspen's culinary scene takes this classic side dish to new heights by infusing the golden fries with truffle oil and sprinkling them with Parmesan cheese. A perfect accompaniment to any meal in this mountain town.

7. Greek-Style Lamb Chops:

Description: Experience the Mediterranean influence in Aspen with Greek-style lamb chops. Succulent lamb, seasoned with Mediterranean herbs and spices, is grilled to perfection. This dish showcases the vibrant and robust flavors of the region, transporting diners to the sun-soaked landscapes of Greece.

6.2 International Flavors in Aspen

Aspen's culinary landscape transcends the boundaries of the Rocky Mountains, welcoming visitors to embark on a global gastronomic journey right in the heart of Colorado. The town's dining establishments seamlessly blend local ingredients with international flavors, offering a diverse and exciting culinary experience.

Asian Fusion Delights:

Aspen's embrace of Asian fusion cuisine is a testament to the town's commitment to diverse and innovative flavors. Visitors can explore a plethora of dishes that beautifully marry traditional Asian recipes with locally sourced ingredients. From sushi rolls featuring fresh mountain trout to miso-glazed black cod, the Asian influence in Aspen's dining scene adds a unique and delicious twist to the mountain experience.

Mediterranean Inspirations:

The Mediterranean influence in Aspen's culinary offerings introduces a burst of sunshine and flavors reminiscent of coastal Europe. Local restaurants showcase dishes like Greek-style lamb chops, Mediterranean seafood paella, and vibrant salads filled with colorful vegetables and olives. The use of local produce elevates these Mediterranean-inspired dishes, creating a harmonious fusion of flavors.

Latin American Influences:

Aspen's diverse palate extends southward, incorporating the lively and spicy notes of Latin American cuisine. Visitors can savor street-style tacos bursting with flavors, Peruvian ceviche made with fresh mountain trout, and empanadas filled with locally sourced ingredients. The town's eateries skillfully blend Latin American culinary traditions with the mountain ambiance, offering a tantalizing culinary experience.

European Elegance:

Aspen's international culinary journey extends to the elegance of European-inspired dishes. Whether indulging in French pastries, Italian pasta creations, or Spanish tapas, visitors can experience the sophistication of European dining right in the heart of the Rocky Mountains. The fusion of classic European techniques with local ingredients creates a dining experience that is both refined and comforting.

Diverse International Cuisines:

Beyond these specific influences, Aspen caters to a wide range of international cuisines. From Indian curries to Middle Eastern delights, the town's restaurants showcase the global diversity that makes Aspen's culinary scene truly exceptional. Visitors can explore a world of flavors without leaving the mountainous embrace of this charming town.

Pairing International Wines and Spirits:

To complement the diverse international flavors, Aspen offers an extensive selection of international wines and spirits. Local sommeliers curate wine lists that span the globe, allowing diners to enhance their culinary experience with the perfect pairing. From French Bordeaux to Argentine Malbec, the wine selection in Aspen reflects the international sophistication of its dining scene.

Aspen's commitment to embracing international flavors not only adds an exciting dimension to the culinary scene but also reflects the town's global perspective and the diverse backgrounds of both residents and visitors.

6.3 Popular Markets and Local Market Adventures

These markets are not just places to shop but hubs of activity, where visitors can engage with locals, sample regional delicacies, and discover unique treasures.

1. Aspen Saturday Market:

One of the highlights of any Aspen visit is the bustling Aspen Saturday Market. This lively event takes place in downtown Aspen, where the streets transform into a vibrant marketplace. Open from June to October, the market showcases a diverse array of offerings. From locally grown fruits and vegetables to handcrafted jewelry, the Aspen Saturday Market is a treasure trove of local delights. Artisans and farmers from the region gather to share their products, creating a dynamic atmosphere that encapsulates the community spirit of Aspen.

2. City Market Aspen:

For those looking to gather ingredients for a mountain-inspired feast, City Market Aspen is a local gem. This grocery store provides an extensive selection of products, including fresh produce, gourmet cheeses, and local wines. It's not just a supermarket; it's a place to discover the culinary essence of Aspen. Visitors can peruse the aisles, finding unique local products and engaging with friendly staff who are often eager to share recommendations for a memorable dining experience.

3. Aspen Farmer's Market:

Held on Saturdays, the Aspen Farmer's Market is a celebration of organic and locally grown produce. Located in the heart of downtown Aspen, this market invites visitors to connect with farmers and vendors offering a diverse range of goods. From farm-fresh fruits and vegetables to artisanal cheeses and handmade crafts, the Aspen Farmer's Market is a sensory delight. It's an opportunity to taste the freshness of the region and appreciate the dedication of local farmers.

4. Local Artisanal Goods:

Aspen's markets aren't just about food; they're also showcases for local artisans and craftspeople. Visitors can explore stalls featuring handmade jewelry, unique artwork, and other crafts that highlight the creativity of the community. Whether you're looking for a distinctive souvenir or a one-of-a-kind gift, Aspen's markets provide a curated selection of artisanal goods that reflect the town's artistic spirit.

5. Aspen's Culinary Scene Comes Alive:

For food enthusiasts, the markets offer a glimpse into Aspen's culinary scene. Local vendors often present a variety of gourmet treats, from artisanal chocolates to freshly baked pastries. It's an opportunity to savor the flavors of Aspen and discover unique delicacies that may not be readily available elsewhere.

6. Engaging with the Community:

The markets in Aspen go beyond commerce; they're a chance to engage with the local community. Residents and vendors alike are often eager to share stories about their products, offer recommendations on the best places to eat, and provide insights into the town's rich history. These interactions add a personal touch to the market experience, creating lasting memories for visitors.

6.4 Dining Etiquette

Understanding the local dining etiquette enhances the enjoyment of the gastronomic journey, ensuring that visitors can fully immerse themselves in the mountain town's sophisticated atmosphere.

1. Reservations Are Paramount:

In Aspen, where popular restaurants draw locals and visitors alike, making reservations is a crucial part of the dining experience. Given the town's popularity, especially during peak seasons, securing a table in advance is highly recommended. This practice not only guarantees a seat but also allows for a more relaxed and enjoyable dining experience, free from the stress of potential long wait times.

2. Tipping Culture:

Tipping is a customary practice in Aspen, reflecting the appreciation for excellent service. When dining in restaurants, it is customary to leave a tip ranging from 15% to 20% of the total bill. Recognizing the hard work of the staff ensures a positive relationship between patrons and the service industry, contributing to the warm and welcoming atmosphere that characterizes Aspen's dining establishments.

3. Dress Code Awareness:

While Aspen is renowned for its laid-back mountain lifestyle, many of its upscale restaurants maintain a smart casual or business casual dress code. It's advisable for visitors to check the specific dress requirements of a chosen restaurant before heading out for a meal. This consideration ensures that diners feel comfortable and align with the ambiance of the dining establishment.

4. Pace Yourself:

Aspen's dining experience is a leisurely affair meant to be savored. Visitors are encouraged to embrace the unhurried pace, allowing ample time to enjoy each course. Rushing through a meal contradicts the laid-back mountain atmosphere, and diners are encouraged to relish the culinary creations and the company in a relaxed manner.

5. Courtesy and Politeness:

The warmth of Aspen extends to its dining establishments, where courtesy and politeness are valued. Simple gestures such as saying "please" and "thank you" contribute to the friendly atmosphere, making the dining experience more enjoyable for both patrons and staff. This respect for one another enhances the overall ambiance of Aspen's restaurants.

6. Children in Dining Establishments:

While Aspen is a family-friendly destination, it's advisable for parents to gauge the atmosphere of a restaurant before bringing young children. Some establishments may have a more formal ambiance, making them better suited for adult diners. Families with children may find more casual dining options to be a comfortable choice.

7. Wine Etiquette:

Given Aspen's appreciation for fine wines, understanding basic wine etiquette can enhance the overall dining experience. If unsure about the wine selection, don't hesitate to seek recommendations from the knowledgeable staff. It's customary to hold the wine glass by the stem to avoid affecting the temperature of the wine.

6.5 Recommended Restaurants with Their Locations

1. The Little Nell - Element 47

Location: 675 East Durant Avenue, Aspen, CO 81611

Description: Nestled within The Little Nell hotel, Element 47 offers an upscale dining experience with a focus on locally sourced ingredients. The menu features modern American cuisine with innovative twists, and the elegant ambiance complements the exquisite culinary offerings.

2. Matsuhisa Aspen

Location: 303 East Main Street, Aspen, CO 81611

Description: Founded by renowned chef Nobu Matsuhisa, Matsuhisa Aspen presents a fusion of traditional Japanese flavors with Peruvian influences. Diners can indulge in a diverse selection of sushi, sashimi, and signature dishes in an intimate and sophisticated setting.

3. Cache Cache

Location: 205 South Mill Street, Aspen, CO 81611

Description: A beloved Aspen institution, Cache Cache is a French-American bistro known for its warm ambiance and exceptional cuisine. The menu boasts a variety of dishes prepared with locally sourced ingredients, creating a delightful fusion of French and American culinary traditions.

4. The White House Tavern

Location: 302 East Hopkins Avenue, Aspen, CO 81611

Description: Combining casual charm with gourmet offerings, The White House Tavern is a local favorite. The menu features gourmet sandwiches, fresh salads, and an extensive selection of craft beers, all served in a historic building with a welcoming atmosphere.

5. Ajax Tavern

Location: 685 East Durant Avenue, Aspen, CO 81611

Description: Located at the base of Aspen Mountain, Ajax Tavern provides a perfect blend of mountain views and a relaxed yet refined atmosphere. The menu offers upscale comfort food, including truffle fries, along with a selection of signature cocktails.

6. Pine Creek Cookhouse

Location: 11399 Castle Creek Road, Aspen, CO 81611

Description: For a unique dining experience amid breathtaking scenery, Pine Creek Cookhouse is nestled in the Castle Creek Valley. Accessible by cross-country skiing or a horse-drawn sleigh ride in winter, it offers hearty mountain cuisine with a focus on local and sustainable ingredients.

7. Jimmy's An American Restaurant & Bar

Location: 205 South Mill Street, Aspen, CO 81611

Description: A staple of Aspen's dining scene, Jimmy's offers a classic American dining experience with a modern twist. Known for its inviting atmosphere and diverse menu, the restaurant features dishes ranging from steaks and seafood to creative cocktails in a vibrant setting.

CHAPTER SEVEN

ENTERTAINMENT AND NIGHTLIFE

7.1 Nightclubs and Lounges with Their Locations

When the sun sets over the picturesque landscapes of Aspen, the vibrant nightlife comes alive with a plethora of nightclubs and lounges that cater to diverse tastes. From chic lounges with crafted cocktails to high-energy nightclubs pulsating with music, Aspen's nightlife scene offers an array of options for those seeking an unforgettable evening.

1. Skybar Aspen

Location: Top of the Aspen Mountain Gondola

Description: Elevate your night at Skybar Aspen, where you'll enjoy handcrafted cocktails with panoramic views of the surrounding mountains. This sophisticated lounge, perched at the summit, offers a unique and unforgettable experience.

2. Bootsy Bellows

Location: Downtown Aspen

Description: Located in the heart of downtown Aspen, Bootsy Bellows is a high-energy nightclub known for its trendy ambiance and live entertainment. It's a favorite among both locals and visitors seeking a lively and upscale atmosphere.

3. Escobar Aspen

Location: Wheeler Opera House Building

Description: Tucked into the historic Wheeler Opera House building, Escobar Aspen provides an intimate and glamorous setting. With a focus on expertly crafted cocktails, it's the perfect venue for those looking to unwind in a more laid-back atmosphere.

4. Chair 9 at The Little Nell

Location: The Little Nell, Slope-side

Description: For a refined après-ski experience that seamlessly transitions into the night, Chair 9 at The Little Nell is a must-visit. This slope-side lounge exudes elegance and warmth, offering a sophisticated space to enjoy signature cocktails.

5. The Red Onion

Location: Cooper Avenue

Description: Steeped in history, The Red Onion stands as one of Aspen's oldest bars. Located on Cooper Avenue, it offers a casual pub atmosphere with live music and a diverse selection of beers. It's a beloved spot for those seeking a blend of tradition and entertainment.

6. Silver Queen Gondola

Location: Base of Aspen Mountain

Description: Providing stunning views, the Silver Queen Gondola offers a unique experience. Whether you're enjoying après-ski drinks or taking in the scenery, this location provides a memorable setting for a night out in Aspen.

7.2 Family-Friendly Entertainment

Aspen isn't just a destination for the adventurous or those seeking a bustling nightlife—it's also a welcoming haven for families looking to create lasting memories together. The town offers a range of family-friendly entertainment options that cater to various ages and interests, ensuring that everyone can find something enjoyable.

1. Aspen Recreation Center (ARC)

Location: 861 Maroon Creek Rd

Description: The Aspen Recreation Center (ARC) is a hub of family-friendly activities. With facilities including ice skating, swimming, and a climbing wall, the ARC provides a diverse range of recreational options for families to enjoy together.

2. Anderson Ranch Arts Center Workshops

Location: 5263 Owl Creek Rd

Description: Families with budding artists or those interested in hands-on activities should explore the workshops at Anderson Ranch Arts Center. The center often hosts family-friendly sessions, allowing parents and children to unleash their creativity together.

3. Aspen Center for Environmental Studies (ACES)

Location: Hallam Lake, 100 Puppy Smith St

Description: For families with a love for nature and wildlife, ACES offers educational and entertaining programs. Guided nature walks, interactive exhibits, and wildlife encounters provide an immersive experience, making learning about the environment an engaging adventure for the whole family.

4. Silver Queen Gondola

Location: Base of Aspen Mountain

Description: A family-friendly activity that offers stunning views, the Silver Queen Gondola provides an opportunity to enjoy Aspen's beauty together. Whether you're heading up for a day of hiking or simply to appreciate the scenery, the gondola ride is an experience the whole family can share.

5. Ute Trail

Location: Trailhead at Ute Ave and Gibson Ave

Description: Hiking the Ute Trail is an outdoor adventure suitable for families. With a moderate level of difficulty, it's accessible for older children, and the reward at the summit includes breathtaking views that everyone can appreciate.

6. Wheeler Opera House

Location: 320 E Hyman Ave

Description: The Wheeler Opera House hosts family-friendly performances and events throughout the year. From children's theater productions to interactive shows, this historic venue offers a cultural experience suitable for all ages.

7.3 Special Events and Festivals

Aspen's vibrant cultural scene is further enriched by a calendar filled with special events and festivals throughout the year. These gatherings not only showcase the town's diverse interests but also offer unique experiences that draw visitors and locals alike. Whether you're a music enthusiast, art lover, or someone seeking to immerse yourself in Aspen's lively atmosphere, the town's events and festivals have something for everyone.

1. Aspen Music Festival and School

Period: Late June to late August

Description: Aspen comes alive with the sounds of classical music during the Aspen Music Festival and School. Renowned musicians and orchestras converge for a summer of enchanting performances, making it a must-attend event for music enthusiasts.

2. Aspen Film Festival

Period: Late September

Description: Cinematic excellence takes center stage at the Aspen Film Festival. Featuring a curated selection of independent films, documentaries, and international cinema, this event offers a diverse and enriching experience for film enthusiasts.

3. Food & Wine Classic in Aspen

Period: Mid-June

Description: Epicureans and culinary aficionados flock to Aspen for the Food & Wine Classic. Renowned chefs, winemakers, and food experts gather for a weekend of tastings, demonstrations, and discussions, transforming Aspen into a gastronomic paradise.

4. Aspen Ideas Festival

Period: Late June to early July

Description: Intellectual stimulation takes the spotlight at the Aspen Ideas Festival. Influential speakers, thinkers, and leaders gather to discuss and explore pressing global issues, fostering conversations that inspire and challenge perspectives.

5. Wintersköl

Period: Late January

Description: Celebrating winter in style, Wintersköl is Aspen's oldest festival, dating back to 1951. This winter carnival features a lively parade, snow sculptures, and a variety of outdoor activities, embracing the joy and beauty of the winter season.

6. Aspen Filmfest

Period: Late September to early October

Description: As autumn sets in, the Aspen Filmfest brings a diverse selection of films to the town. Movie enthusiasts can enjoy thought-provoking narratives and engage with filmmakers during this captivating fall event.

CHAPTER EIGHT

CULTURAL EXPERIENCES

8.1 Museums and Galleries

Aspen, a city known for its natural beauty and outdoor adventures, also boasts a rich cultural scene with its diverse array of museums and galleries. These institutions offer visitors a unique opportunity to delve into the art, history, and cultural heritage that shape the identity of this vibrant mountain community.

One standout destination is the Aspen Art Museum (AAM), a contemporary art space that has become a focal point for artistic expression in the region. The museum, designed by architect Shigeru Ban, is not only an architectural marvel but also a testament to Aspen's commitment to promoting and engaging with modern art. Inside, visitors can explore thought-provoking exhibitions featuring a mix of local, national, and international artists. The AAM's dedication to fostering a dynamic cultural environment is evident in its diverse range of programs, from artist talks to interactive installations.

For those intrigued by Aspen's historical roots, the Aspen Historical Society offers a captivating journey through time. The society operates multiple sites, including the Wheeler/Stallard Museum and the Holden/Marolt Mining & Ranching Museum. The Wheeler/Stallard Museum, housed in a beautifully preserved Victorian mansion, showcases Aspen's transformation from a mining town to a cultural hub. Meanwhile, the Holden/Marolt Mining & Ranching

Museum provides a hands-on experience, allowing visitors to explore the region's mining and ranching history through exhibits and outdoor displays.

Art enthusiasts looking for a more intimate setting will find solace in Aspen's many galleries. Baldwin Gallery, located in the heart of downtown Aspen, is a premier contemporary art space showcasing works by both established and emerging artists. The gallery's curated exhibitions span various mediums, including painting, sculpture, and photography, providing a comprehensive snapshot of the current art landscape.

In addition to contemporary art, Aspen celebrates its Western heritage at the Society of the West gallery. This gallery immerses visitors in the artistic expressions of the American West, featuring works that capture the spirit of the region. From Native American art to depictions of cowboy culture, the Society of the West adds a unique dimension to Aspen's cultural tapestry.

8.2 Cultural Arts and Heritage

Beyond the walls of museums and galleries, Aspen's cultural arts and heritage thrive in various forms, enriching the visitor experience with a deeper understanding of the community's roots and ongoing traditions.

The Aspen Music Festival and School stands as a testament to the city's commitment to nurturing musical talent and appreciation. Founded in 1949, this internationally renowned festival brings together exceptional musicians and students for a summer of performances spanning classical, contemporary, and chamber music. The festival not only contributes to Aspen's cultural vibrancy but also allows visitors to partake in the joy of live musical performances set against the stunning backdrop of the Rocky Mountains.

Aspen's commitment to the arts extends to the theatrical realm with the historic Wheeler Opera House. Constructed during the silver mining boom, the Wheeler has undergone renovations to become a premier venue for performing arts. Today, visitors can enjoy a diverse range of events, from live theater productions to concerts and film screenings. The Wheeler Opera House serves as a cultural anchor, fostering a sense of community through shared artistic experiences.

For a deeper dive into Aspen's history and heritage, the Aspen Chapel provides a serene space for reflection. The chapel, surrounded by lush gardens, serves as both a spiritual sanctuary and a venue for cultural events. With its picturesque setting and commitment to fostering a sense of community, the Aspen Chapel encapsulates the essence of Aspen's cultural and spiritual identity.

8.3 Understanding Local Customs and Traditions

To truly appreciate the fabric of Aspen's community, visitors are encouraged to understand and engage with the local customs and traditions that define this unique mountain town.

Aspen's residents take pride in their commitment to environmental sustainability and outdoor recreation. It's not uncommon to see locals actively participating in activities such as hiking, biking, and skiing. This emphasis on a healthy and active lifestyle contributes to the city's overall vibrancy and serves as an inspiration for visitors looking to immerse themselves in the local way of life.

The appreciation for the arts is deeply ingrained in Aspen's culture. Locals actively support the numerous galleries, museums, and cultural events that contribute to the city's artistic landscape. Visitors are often welcomed to join in these celebrations, whether it's attending gallery openings, live performances, or cultural festivals that showcase Aspen's creative spirit.

Aspen's culinary scene reflects a commitment to locally sourced and sustainable ingredients. The farm-to-table movement is embraced by many restaurants, and visitors can savor the flavors of the region while supporting local farmers and producers. Engaging in conversations with locals about their favorite eateries or attending food festivals provides an excellent opportunity to connect with Aspen's culinary traditions.

Community events play a significant role in Aspen's social fabric. Whether it's the annual Winterskol Festival celebrating winter sports or the Aspen Ideas Festival fostering intellectual discussions, these gatherings showcase the communal spirit that defines Aspen. Visitors are encouraged to check local event calendars and participate in these festivities to gain a deeper understanding of the community's values and traditions.

8.4 Souvenirs and Mementos

1. Handcrafted Aspen Jewelry:

Description: Bring home a piece of Aspen's natural beauty with handcrafted jewelry inspired by the surrounding landscapes. Look for pieces made with materials like sterling silver and locally sourced stones, capturing the essence of the mountains in every intricate design. Whether it's a delicate pendant or a bold statement piece, Aspen jewelry serves as a timeless and elegant souvenir.

2. Local Art Prints and Photography:

Description: Commemorate your Aspen experience by investing in local art prints or photography capturing the stunning landscapes, vibrant cultural scenes, and architectural marvels of the city. Many galleries and gift shops offer limited edition prints by Aspen artists, allowing you to take home a visual representation of the unique charm that defines the mountain town.

3. Aspen-Inspired Gourmet Treats:

Description: Indulge your taste buds with gourmet treats inspired by Aspen's culinary scene. Look for locally produced items such as artisanal chocolates, small-batch jams, and specialty cheeses. These delectable treats not only make for delightful souvenirs but also offer a delicious reminder of Aspen's commitment to quality and sustainability in its culinary offerings.

4. Aspen-themed Apparel and Accessories:

Description: Show off your Aspen spirit with apparel and accessories featuring the city's iconic symbols and motifs. Look for t-shirts, hoodies, and hats adorned with Aspen's mountain skyline or ski-related designs. Additionally, explore boutique stores for unique accessories like scarves, gloves, and beanies that reflect the city's stylish and outdoor-oriented culture.

5. Local Artisan Pottery and Ceramics:

Description: Discover the craftsmanship of local artisans with handcrafted pottery and ceramics that embody Aspen's rustic charm. From mugs and bowls to decorative pieces, these items often showcase unique glazes and textures inspired by the surrounding natural beauty. Bringing home a piece of functional art allows you to enjoy Aspen's artistic flair in your everyday life.

CHAPTER NINE

OUTDOOR ACTIVITIES

9.1 Skiing or Snowboarding on Aspen Mountain:

Aspen Mountain stands as an iconic symbol of world-class skiing and snowboarding, inviting enthusiasts to a thrilling adventure amidst breathtaking landscapes. The allure of this winter wonderland extends beyond its challenging terrain to embrace both seasoned professionals and those taking their first slide down the snowy slopes.

For seasoned pros, Aspen Mountain offers a challenging playground characterized by steep descents, mogul runs, and gladed tree areas. The Silver Queen Gondola whisks skiers and snowboarders to the summit, where they are greeted by panoramic views of the Elk Mountains. As you carve through the meticulously groomed trails, you'll feel the exhilaration of navigating the same terrain that has hosted elite competitions and earned Aspen its reputation as a premier winter sports destination.

Novice enthusiasts need not feel left out, as Aspen Mountain boasts beginner-friendly areas and a variety of lessons tailored to different skill levels. Gentle slopes near the base provide a perfect training ground for those stepping onto skis or strapping into a snowboard for the first time. Expert instructors are on hand to guide beginners through the basics, ensuring a safe and enjoyable introduction to the world of alpine sports.

The après-ski culture at Aspen Mountain is as enticing as its slopes. After an invigorating day on the mountain, skiers and snowboarders can unwind at one of the cozy lodges or vibrant mountain restaurants. Savor gourmet cuisine, sip on locally crafted beverages, and share stories of your alpine exploits with fellow enthusiasts. The nightlife in Aspen adds another layer to the experience, with a variety of entertainment options ranging from live music to intimate gatherings.

9.2 Hiking the Maroon Bells Scenic Trail:

Embark on a journey through nature's masterpiece by hiking the Maroon Bells Scenic Trail, an experience that transcends the ordinary and immerses you in the awe-inspiring beauty of the Colorado Rockies. The Maroon Bells, two towering peaks reflected in the crystalline Maroon Lake, form a postcard-perfect scene that beckons both casual strollers and avid hikers.

The trail, meandering through alpine meadows and dense forests, offers varying difficulty levels, ensuring that every nature enthusiast can find a path that suits their preferences. For those seeking a leisurely stroll, there are well-maintained paths around Maroon Lake, providing ample opportunities to capture the iconic reflection of the Bells in the water.

As you ascend into higher elevations, the landscape becomes more rugged, presenting challenges for hikers craving a more strenuous adventure. Numerous switchbacks and rocky outcrops lead to vantage points that unveil sweeping vistas of the surrounding wilderness. The crisp mountain air, the scent of pine, and the melodic sounds of nature create a sensory symphony that accompanies your every step.

The Maroon Bells Scenic Trail is not merely a physical journey; it's a visual feast. Wildflowers carpet the landscape in a vibrant tapestry of colors during the warmer months, and the changing foliage paints the hillsides with hues of gold and crimson in the fall. Wildlife, including marmots, deer, and the occasional elk, adds an element of enchantment to the hike.

For photography enthusiasts, the Maroon Bells present an ever-changing canvas of light and shadow. Sunrise and sunset are particularly magical, casting the peaks in warm, golden hues and transforming the surrounding landscapes into a photographer's dream.

Whether you're seeking a peaceful communion with nature or a challenging trek to test your limits, the Maroon Bells Scenic Trail stands ready to offer an unforgettable hiking experience, leaving you with memories etched against the backdrop of one of nature's most sublime creations.

9.3 Mountain Biking in Snowmass Bike Park:

For those who crave the thrill of downhill adventures and the rush of wind against their faces, Snowmass Bike Park emerges as the ultimate playground for mountain biking enthusiasts. Nestled within the stunning landscapes of the Elk Mountains, this bike park offers an adrenaline-fueled experience for riders of all skill levels.

The park boasts an extensive network of trails, carefully designed to cater to beginners, intermediate riders, and seasoned experts. From flowy descents through alpine meadows to technical downhill sections weaving through dense forests, Snowmass Bike Park delivers a diverse range of terrains to keep every rider engaged.

Novice bikers can hone their skills on gently rolling trails near the base, where wide berms and gradual descents provide a supportive environment for building confidence. Meanwhile, experienced riders can tackle challenging features, drops, and jumps that characterize the more advanced trails, ensuring an exhilarating experience for those seeking an adrenaline rush.

Snowmass Bike Park is not only renowned for its diverse trails but also for its stunning mountain vistas. As riders navigate the twists and turns of the downhill trails, they are treated to panoramic views of Snowmass Village, the Roaring Fork Valley, and the surrounding peaks. The immersive experience of hurtling down the mountain while surrounded by the grandeur of nature creates a symbiotic connection between rider and landscape.

The park's commitment to inclusivity extends to its rental and lesson offerings, making it accessible for those who may be new to the sport. Knowledgeable instructors are available to guide riders through the basics or help them refine their techniques, ensuring a safe and enjoyable mountain biking experience.

After a day of conquering the trails, riders can relax and share their stories at the base area. Snowmass Village offers a vibrant après-bike scene, with local breweries and eateries providing the perfect backdrop for recounting the day's adventures. The camaraderie among fellow bikers, combined with the stunning surroundings, creates an atmosphere that lingers long after the bikes are parked.

9.4 Fly Fishing in the Roaring Fork River:

Immerse yourself in the rhythmic dance between angler and river as you embark on a fly-fishing adventure along the renowned Roaring Fork River. Nestled within the heart of Aspen, this pristine waterway offers not only a tranquil escape but also a chance to connect with nature in one of the most picturesque settings imaginable.

The Roaring Fork River is renowned for its clear waters, teeming with various trout species that entice anglers from novice to expert. Whether you're a seasoned fly-fisher looking for a challenge or a beginner eager to learn the art of casting, the river provides an idyllic setting for a day of angling.

As you wade into the river, surrounded by the soothing sounds of flowing water and rustling leaves, the immersive experience begins. The Roaring Fork is a freestone river, known for its diverse habitats ranging from riffles and pools to deep runs, providing an array of fishing environments for anglers to explore.

The riverbanks are adorned with lush vegetation, creating a natural haven for wildlife. Keep an eye out for bald eagles soaring overhead, beavers building their dams, and deer venturing to the water's edge for a drink. The Roaring Fork

River not only offers a sanctuary for trout but also serves as a vital corridor for the region's diverse ecosystem.

Local fly-fishing guides, with their intimate knowledge of the river's nuances, are available to enhance your fishing experience. They can lead you to the most promising spots, share insights into the behavior of the river's inhabitants, and provide valuable tips on the art of fly fishing. Guided excursions cater to both individuals and groups, ensuring that everyone, from families to solo adventurers, can enjoy the pleasures of this outdoor pursuit.

The Roaring Fork Valley's commitment to conservation has ensured the sustainability of its rivers, making catch-and-release practices essential for preserving the delicate balance of the ecosystem. Anglers are not only participating in a beloved pastime but also contributing to the preservation of this natural treasure for generations to come.

After a day spent casting lines and connecting with the river's rhythm, anglers can retreat to the charming town of Aspen to share tales of the day's catches. Local eateries often feature delectable trout dishes, allowing anglers to savor the fruits of their labor in a culinary celebration of the river's bounty.

9.5 Hot Air Balloon Ride Over Aspen Valley:

Elevate your perspective and embark on a soaring adventure above the picturesque landscapes of the Aspen Valley with a hot air balloon ride. This unique and memorable experience promises unparalleled views of the mountains, valleys, and rivers that define this enchanting region.

As the balloon gently ascends, you'll find yourself suspended in a basket beneath a vibrant canopy, drifting silently through the crisp mountain air. The ascent is gradual, allowing for a smooth transition from solid ground to the expansive skies. Once airborne, the quietude of the experience creates a sense of serenity, offering a stark contrast to the adrenaline-fueled activities on the ground.

The panoramic views from the hot air balloon are nothing short of spectacular. The Elk Mountains, with their majestic peaks, provide a stunning backdrop, while the Roaring Fork River winds its way through the valley below. Aspen's lush landscapes unfold like a patchwork quilt, revealing dense forests, alpine meadows, and charming townships.

The changing colors of the landscape, particularly during sunrise or sunset flights, add a magical quality to the experience. The soft hues of dawn or dusk cast long shadows over the mountains, creating a visual symphony of warm tones that dance across the scenery. Balloon rides during these times are especially popular for capturing breathtaking photographs that encapsulate the beauty of Aspen Valley.

Hot air balloon rides offer a sense of tranquility and freedom, providing a unique vantage point that allows passengers to appreciate the interconnectedness of nature. The pilot, skilled in navigating the winds, ensures a safe and enjoyable journey, pointing out notable landmarks and sharing insights into the geography and history of the region.

Each hot air balloon ride is a distinctive experience, influenced by the prevailing winds and the pilot's chosen route. Some flights may take you over the charming town of

Aspen, offering a bird's-eye view of its architectural gems and vibrant streets. Others might carry you across the undulating hillsides, providing a perspective of the wilderness that few get to witness.

Upon landing, typically met with a gentle touch, passengers often share a celebratory toast to the adventure with a glass of champagne. The camaraderie among fellow balloon enthusiasts and the shared sense of awe at the beauty witnessed from above create lasting memories that linger long after the balloon has been packed away.

Whether you choose a sunrise flight to witness the world waking up or a sunset journey to bid the day farewell, a hot air balloon ride over Aspen Valley is an experience that transcends the ordinary. It's a poetic dance between earth and sky, a celebration of nature's grandeur, and a journey that leaves an indelible mark on the hearts of those fortunate enough to partake in this airborne escapade.

CHAPTER TEN

ASPEN TRAVEL ITINERARIES

10.1 One-Week Highlights Tour

Day 1: Welcome to Aspen

Arrive in Aspen and check into your chosen accommodation, whether it's a luxury resort, a cozy bed and breakfast, or a boutique hotel.

Spend the afternoon exploring downtown Aspen. Wander through the charming streets, visit boutique shops, and immerse yourself in the local culture.

Evening: Indulge in a welcome dinner at one of Aspen's renowned restaurants, experiencing the town's diverse culinary offerings.

Day 2: Cultural Immersion

Morning: Begin your day with a visit to the Aspen Art Museum. Explore contemporary art exhibits and engage with the vibrant art scene.

Afternoon: Dive into Aspen's rich history at the Aspen Historical Society. Gain insights into the town's mining origins and development over the years.

Evening: Enjoy a leisurely dinner at a local restaurant, sharing stories and impressions from your first day in Aspen.

Day 3: Maroon Bells Exploration

Morning: Embark on a day trip to the Maroon Bells, Aspen's iconic twin peaks. Hike the scenic trails or simply take in the breathtaking views of the surrounding landscapes.

Afternoon: Picnic at one of the alpine lakes near Maroon Bells, surrounded by nature's grandeur.

Evening: Return to Aspen and choose a cozy spot for dinner, recounting the day's adventures.

Day 4: Aspen Mountain Adventure

Morning: If visiting during the winter, hit the slopes of Aspen Mountain for a day of skiing or snowboarding. In the summer, explore hiking and mountain biking trails.

Afternoon: Take a break at one of the mountain's lodges or restaurants, savoring the alpine atmosphere.

Evening: Dine in Aspen's downtown, choosing a restaurant with a view or a cozy setting, depending on your mood.

Day 5: Scenic Drive and Independence Pass

Morning: Embark on a scenic drive along Independence Pass, capturing panoramic views of the mountains and valleys.

Afternoon: Explore downtown Aspen for some shopping or visit an art gallery.

Evening: Enjoy a relaxed dinner at one of the local eateries, savoring the flavors of Aspen.

Day 6: Culinary Delights

Morning: Take a leisurely morning stroll through Aspen, perhaps visiting a local coffee shop for a caffeine boost.

Afternoon: Dive into Aspen's culinary scene for lunch, trying dishes that showcase the town's diverse flavors.

Evening: Indulge in a fine dining experience at one of Aspen's top restaurants, immersing yourself in the gastronomic delights the town has to offer.

Day 7: Farewell to Aspen

Morning: Before departing, consider a morning hike to soak in the natural beauty once more or indulge in a leisurely brunch.

Afternoon: Take some time to reflect on your week in Aspen. Consider revisiting a favorite spot or discovering a new one.

Evening: Bid farewell to Aspen with a heart full of memories. Depart with the promise to return and explore more of this captivating mountain town.

10.2 Weekend Getaway

This meticulously crafted day-by-day itinerary ensures you make the most of your short but magical retreat in this alpine paradise.

Day 1: Friday - Arrival and Downtown Delights

Morning: Arrival in Aspen

As you touch down in Aspen, the crisp mountain air welcomes you to this picturesque destination. Check into your chosen accommodation, whether it's a luxury resort, a cozy bed and breakfast, or a boutique hotel in downtown Aspen.

Afternoon: Downtown Exploration

Kick off your weekend adventure with a leisurely stroll through downtown Aspen. Immerse yourself in the vibrant atmosphere as you explore boutique shops, art galleries, and charming cafes. Stop for a delightful lunch at one of the local eateries, savoring the first flavors of Aspen.

Evening: Sunset at Smuggler Mountain

As the sun begins its descent, embark on a scenic hike to Smuggler Mountain. The trail offers panoramic views of Aspen and the surrounding mountains, creating a perfect backdrop for a romantic sunset. Capture the breathtaking hues of the sky as the day transitions into evening.

Night: Dinner in Town

Head back to downtown Aspen for a delectable dinner at one of the town's renowned restaurants. Whether you choose a fine dining experience or opt for a cozy chalet-style eatery, let the evening unfold with delicious cuisine and the charming ambiance of Aspen.

Day 2: Saturday - Alpine Adventures

Morning: Breakfast at the Base of Aspen Mountain

Start your day with a hearty breakfast at a cafe near the base of Aspen Mountain. Fuel up for a day filled with alpine adventures.

Late Morning: Gondola Ride and Hiking on Aspen Mountain

Take a scenic gondola ride to the top of Aspen Mountain, known locally as Ajax. Revel in the breathtaking views as you ascend. Once at the summit, explore the hiking trails, offering varying difficulty levels. Capture the mountain vistas and enjoy the serenity of the alpine surroundings.

Afternoon: Lunch and Exploring Aspen Highlands

Descend from Aspen Mountain and treat yourself to a leisurely lunch in town. In the afternoon, venture to Aspen Highlands for more outdoor exploration. Hike, bike, or simply soak in the mountain ambiance at this renowned destination.

Evening: Dinner and Cultural Experience

As the day winds down, indulge in a well-deserved dinner at a restaurant of your choice. Consider attending a cultural event or performance at The Wheeler Opera House for a touch of sophistication and entertainment to cap off your Saturday night.

Day 3: Sunday - Nature and Relaxation

Morning: Maroon Bells Exploration

On your final day in Aspen, dedicate the morning to exploring the iconic Maroon Bells. Whether you choose to hike the scenic trails or simply admire the view from the lakeside, the Maroon Bells offer a tranquil and awe-inspiring experience.

Late Morning: Brunch in Nature

After your Maroon Bells adventure, enjoy a leisurely brunch in the midst of nature. Pack a picnic or visit a local eatery with outdoor seating to savor delicious bites surrounded by the beauty of Aspen.

Afternoon: Relaxation and Spa Time

Conclude your weekend getaway with an afternoon of relaxation. Consider indulging in spa treatments at one of Aspen's luxury spas, unwinding in hot tubs, or simply enjoying the serene ambiance of your surroundings.

Evening: Farewell Dinner and Stargazing

As the sun sets on your Aspen getaway, savor a farewell dinner at a cozy restaurant. Afterward, if weather permits, head to a stargazing spot outside of town. Aspen's clear mountain skies offer a spectacular view of the stars, providing a magical end to your weekend retreat.

10.3 Family-Friendly Adventure

Day 1: Arrival and Downtown Delight

Arrive in Aspen and settle into your chosen family-friendly accommodation. Begin your adventure with a leisurely exploration of downtown Aspen. Stroll along the charming streets, adorned with boutique shops and cozy cafes. Engage the family in choosing a unique restaurant for dinner, setting the tone for culinary exploration throughout your stay.

Day 2: Aspen Art and Historical Immersion

Immerse your family in Aspen's cultural tapestry on day two. Start at the Aspen Art Museum, where contemporary art awaits. Explore interactive exhibits that captivate both young and adult art enthusiasts. Follow this with a visit to the Aspen Historical Society, offering a fascinating journey through the town's mining origins and evolution. Share stories of Aspen's past, creating a connection with the town's history.

Day 3: Nature's Playground at Maroon Bells

Escape into the great outdoors with a visit to the iconic Maroon Bells. Opt for a family-friendly hike along one of the scenic trails, allowing the children to experience the thrill of exploration surrounded by nature's grandeur. Capture the magic of the twin peaks through family photographs and enjoy a picnic amidst the serene landscapes.

Day 4: Adventure Awaits on Aspen Mountain

Head to Aspen Mountain (Ajax) for a day of family-friendly adventure. In the winter months, partake in skiing or snowboarding suitable for all skill levels. In the summer, explore the mountain's hiking and biking trails, ensuring there are activities catering to every family member's preference. Conclude the day with a shared sense of accomplishment and perhaps a family-friendly aprés-ski experience.

Day 5: Ute Trail and Hunter Creek Exploration

Discover more of Aspen's outdoor wonders on day five. Embark on a family-friendly hike along the Ute Trail, providing breathtaking views of the Elk Mountain Range and

Roaring Fork Valley. Follow this with an exploration of Hunter Creek Trail, a secluded path perfect for family bonding amidst nature's beauty.

Day 6: Culinary Adventures in Aspen

Dedicate this day to culinary exploration, allowing the family to savor the diverse flavors of Aspen. Choose family-friendly restaurants that offer a mix of local and international cuisine. From cozy chalet-style eateries to casual dining spots, let each family member indulge in their preferred culinary delights. Consider an evening of cooking together or attending a family-friendly cooking class for a unique culinary adventure.

Day 7: Snowmass Village Excursion

Take a short drive to Snowmass Village for a change of scenery. In the winter, indulge in family-friendly skiing and snow activities, while the summer offers hiking and outdoor adventures suitable for all ages. Explore the vibrant events and attractions of Snowmass Village, creating shared memories outside the heart of Aspen.

Day 8: Wheeler Opera House and Cultural Connection

Immerse the family in Aspen's cultural scene on day eight. Attend a family-friendly performance at the historic Wheeler Opera House, where live entertainment captivates audiences of all ages. Engage in conversations about the arts, fostering a deeper connection with the cultural fabric of Aspen.

Day 9: Family Recreation at Aspen Recreation Center

Experience family-friendly recreation at the Aspen Recreation Center. The facility offers pools, ice skating, and various activities suitable for all ages. Enjoy a day of laughter, games, and shared moments, creating a unique blend of family recreation in the heart of Aspen.

Day 10: Farewell Reflections

As your family-friendly adventure in Aspen draws to a close, take the final day to reflect on the experiences shared. Consider revisiting a favorite spot, be it a downtown café, a scenic trail, or a cultural landmark. Capture the essence of your family getaway with a final family photo, immortalizing the memories created in the heart of the mountains.

10.4 Solo Traveler's Journey

Day 1-3: Independent Exploration of Downtown Aspen

Upon arrival in Aspen, take the first day to settle in and acclimate to the mountain atmosphere. Wander through the charming streets of downtown Aspen, exploring the boutique shops, art galleries, and quaint cafes. Absorb the artistic and cultural nuances at your own pace, reveling in the freedom to choose your path.

Visit the Aspen Art Museum, where contemporary art becomes a companion on your solo journey. Allow the exhibits to spark introspective moments as you connect with the artistic expressions showcased in this cultural hub. In the evening, dine at a local restaurant, immersing yourself in the flavors of Aspen.

On Day 2, continue your exploration of downtown Aspen, discovering hidden gems and capturing the town's essence through your lens. Visit the Aspen Historical Society to delve into the mining origins and rich history of this mountain town. Engage in conversations with locals, fostering connections that add depth to your solo adventure.

Day 4-7: Nature Retreat and Outdoor Adventures

As your solo journey continues, venture into the embrace of nature. On Day 4, set out for the iconic Maroon Bells. The scenic trails offer a perfect introduction to Aspen's natural beauty. Whether you choose a challenging hike or a leisurely stroll, let the mountains become your companions.

Extend your outdoor escapades on Day 5 with a visit to Aspen Mountain (Ajax). Depending on the season, engage in activities that resonate with your spirit – ski down powdery slopes in winter or hike and mountain bike in the warmer months. Revel in the freedom of choosing your adventure.

On Day 6, explore the less frequented trails of Smuggler Mountain. The solitude of this trail provides a perfect backdrop for introspection. Allow the rhythm of your footsteps to synchronize with the beating heart of nature. Day 7 invites you to Hunter Creek Trail, another hidden gem offering serenity and scenic vistas for your solo exploration.

Day 8-10: Culinary Experiences and Cultural Connection

Transition into a more relaxed phase of your solo journey by indulging in Aspen's culinary delights. On Day 8, embark on a culinary adventure, trying unique dishes and flavors. Choose cozy chalet-style restaurants or explore the local pub scene, savoring meals at your own pace.

Day 9 offers a cultural interlude at The Wheeler Opera House. Attend a performance or simply admire the architectural beauty of this historic venue. Engage in conversations with fellow culture enthusiasts or relish the solo experience of absorbing the arts.

As your culinary exploration continues on Day 10, visit Woody Creek Tavern. This historic watering hole not only offers hearty meals but also a glimpse into Aspen's past. Share stories with locals or enjoy a quiet meal reflecting on the cultural tapestry surrounding you.

Day 11-14: Reflect and Recharge

As your solo journey in Aspen nears its conclusion, dedicate the final days to personal reflection and relaxation. On Day 11, choose serene spots like the John Denver Sanctuary for moments of contemplation. Allow the beauty of the surroundings to inspire thoughts and reflections on your solo adventure.

Day 12 invites you to unwind at the Aspen Recreation Center. Whether you choose to take a dip in the pools, enjoy a session of ice skating, or simply relax in the surroundings, let this be a day of leisure and recharging.

10.5 Romantic Getaways
Day 1: Arrival and Downtown Delights

Morning:

Arrive in Aspen and check into your chosen romantic retreat. Begin your getaway with a leisurely morning, perhaps indulging in a cozy breakfast in bed or on a private balcony with views of the surrounding mountains.

Afternoon:

Stroll hand in hand through downtown Aspen. Explore the charming boutiques, art galleries, and cafes that line the streets. Take your time to discover unique treasures and enjoy a light lunch at a quaint cafe, soaking in the romantic ambiance   of   the   town.

Evening:

For a romantic dinner, choose one of Aspen's intimate restaurants. Opt for a cozy chalet-style eatery where you can share delectable dishes and raise a toast to the start of your romantic escape.

Day 2: Artistic Romance and Cultural Connection

Morning:

Savor a lazy morning together, perhaps with breakfast at a local bakery or in the comfort of your accommodation. Allow the day to unfold at a relaxed pace, reveling in each other's company.

Afternoon:

Immerse yourselves in the world of art at the Aspen Art Museum. Wander through the exhibits hand in hand, appreciating the creativity and sparking conversations inspired by the artwork.

Evening:

Dine at a restaurant with a romantic ambiance, sharing stories and laughter over a delightful dinner. Consider attending a performance at The Wheeler Opera House, where the cultural vibrancy of Aspen comes to life in a charming setting.

Day 3: Nature's Embrace at Maroon Bells

Morning:

Embark on a romantic adventure to the iconic Maroon Bells. Pack a picnic basket with your favorite treats and hike the scenic trails hand in hand. Find a secluded spot to enjoy a romantic picnic with the breathtaking twin peaks as your backdrop.

Afternoon:

Capture the magic of Maroon Bells through photographs that will forever encapsulate the romance of the moment. Spend the afternoon exploring the area, reveling in the natural beauty that surrounds you.

Evening:

Return to Aspen for a romantic dinner at a restaurant with mountain views. Reflect on the day's adventures and savor the connection you've deepened amidst the stunning landscapes.

Day 4: Shared Adventures on Aspen Mountain

Morning:

Whether covered in snow or bathed in sunshine, Aspen Mountain beckons for a day of shared adventures. In winter, hit the slopes for a day of skiing or snowboarding. In the summer, explore the mountain's hiking and biking trails, reveling in the alpine beauty.

Afternoon:

Pause for a romantic mountainside picnic, enjoying each other's company amidst the fresh mountain air. The panoramic views from Aspen Mountain create a perfect backdrop for moments of connection and shared joy.

Evening:

As the day winds down, unwind at a cozy chalet-style restaurant. Share a decadent dessert and toast to the adventures you've undertaken together on Aspen Mountain.

Day 5: Culinary Delights and Evening Romance

Morning:

Begin the day with a leisurely breakfast, perhaps opting for a spot that offers both delicious cuisine and a romantic atmosphere. Allow the morning to unfold with shared laughter and quiet moments.

Afternoon:

Explore Aspen's culinary scene further with a culinary tour or by visiting local markets. Sample artisanal treats and gather ingredients for a romantic evening meal.

Evening:

Cook a romantic dinner together in the privacy of your accommodation or opt for a cooking class to enhance your culinary skills. Share a bottle of wine, indulge in delicious flavors, and relish the intimate moments created through the joy of shared cooking.

Day 6: Tranquil Reflections and Cultural Experiences

Morning:

Choose a serene spot, perhaps at the John Denver Sanctuary, for moments of tranquil reflection. Enjoy a quiet morning together, connecting with nature and each other.

Afternoon:

Engage in a cultural experience, whether it's attending a local event, exploring art galleries, or simply wandering through downtown Aspen. Allow the day to unfold spontaneously, embracing the cultural richness of the town.

Evening:

Conclude the day with a romantic dinner at a venue known for its intimate ambiance. Share your reflections on the trip and relish the deepened connection forged through cultural exploration.

Day 7: Departure with Hearts Full of Memories

Morning:

On your final morning in Aspen, savor a leisurely breakfast together. Take a moment to express gratitude for the romantic getaway and reminisce about the unforgettable moments shared.

Afternoon:

Before departure, take a scenic drive or a final stroll through downtown Aspen. Purchase a small keepsake to symbolize your time in this mountain paradise.

Evening:

As you bid farewell to Aspen, carry with you the cherished memories of a romantic escape filled with love, laughter, and shared adventures. Depart with hearts full and a promise to return to this enchanting destination.

CHAPTER ELEVEN

PRACTICAL TIPS AND RESOURCES

11.1 local phrases and vocabulary

Whether you're hitting the slopes, exploring the town, or enjoying the après-ski scene, incorporating these local phrases into your conversations will make you feel like a true Aspenite.

1. Pow Day:

- Usage: "Hey, looks like tomorrow is a pow day! Grab your skis, and let's make the most of that fresh powder."
- Meaning: Refers to a day with abundant, powdery snow—a term that sparks excitement among skiers and snowboarders gearing up for ideal slope conditions.

2. Après-Ski:

- Usage: "The best part of the day is après-ski. Let's head to the base and enjoy some drinks and live music at Aspen Brewing Company."
- Meaning: Describes the socializing and entertainment that follows a day of skiing or snowboarding, often celebrated at local bars and establishments.

3. Gondola:

- Usage: "Meet me at the gondola for an early morning ride up Ajax. The views are spectacular, especially during sunrise."
- Meaning: Refers to the cable car used to transport individuals up the mountains. The gondola is not just a mode of transportation but a quintessential Aspen experience.

4. Bluebird Day:

- Usage: "Tomorrow is forecasted to be a bluebird day! Perfect for a hike or enjoying a leisurely stroll through downtown."
- Meaning: Describes a day with clear blue skies and sunshine, creating optimal weather conditions for outdoor activities in Aspen.

5. High Altitude Cuisine:

- Usage: "Aspen's culinary scene is all about high altitude cuisine. You can taste the freshness and unique flavors in every dish."
- Meaning: Refers to the local approach to cooking, taking into account the high-altitude conditions. The cuisine often features locally sourced ingredients.

6. Farm-to-Table:

- Usage: "Have you tried the new farm-to-table restaurant on Mill Street? Their menu changes with the seasons, highlighting local produce."

- Meaning: Emphasizes the use of fresh, locally sourced ingredients in restaurants. Aspen's farm-to-table establishments showcase a commitment to sustainable and seasonal dining.

7. Locavore:

- Usage: "Aspen attracts a lot of locavores who appreciate the region's farmers and producers. It's inspiring to see such dedication to local flavors."
- Meaning: Describes individuals who prioritize consuming locally produced food. Aspen's locavore community supports regional agriculture and sustainable practices.

8. The Sundeck:

- Usage: "Let's take a break at The Sundeck. It's not just about the food; the panoramic views up there are absolutely breathtaking."
- Meaning: Refers to a popular on-mountain restaurant known for its scenic views. The Sundeck is a favorite spot for both culinary experiences and mountain vistas.

9. The Belly Up:

- Usage: "The Belly Up is the heartbeat of Aspen's nightlife. We should catch a live show there—it's always a memorable experience."
- Meaning: Refers to a renowned live music venue in Aspen. The Belly Up is synonymous with the lively and diverse music scene in the town.

11.2 Emergency Contacts

Understanding who to contact in various situations can ensure a swift and effective response to any unforeseen circumstances.

1. Emergency Services:

Emergency Services (Police, Fire, Medical): 911

In the event of a life-threatening emergency, dial 911. This universal emergency number connects you to the local police, fire, and medical services. Provide accurate details about your location and the nature of the emergency for prompt assistance.

2. Local Hospitals:

Aspen Valley Hospital:

For non-emergency medical situations, Aspen Valley Hospital is your primary point of contact. Equipped with comprehensive healthcare services, the hospital caters to both residents and visitors. Save their contact information for any unexpected health concerns.

3. Mountain Rescue:

Mountain Rescue Aspen:

Aspen's mountainous terrain offers thrilling adventures but can also pose challenges. If you find yourself in need of assistance while exploring the backcountry or hiking trails, contact Mountain Rescue Aspen. Their skilled team specializes in mountain search and rescue operations.

4. Ski Patrol:

Aspen Snowmass Ski Patrol:

For emergencies on the slopes, the Aspen Snowmass Ski Patrol is your dedicated resource. Whether you encounter difficulties while skiing or snowboarding, the ski patrol is trained to handle situations specific to mountain recreation.

5. Non-Emergency Assistance:

Aspen Police Department (Non-Emergency):

Not all situations require immediate emergency response, but you may still need assistance. In such cases, contact the non-emergency line of the Aspen Police Department. They can provide information, guidance, and support for non-urgent matters.

11.3 Sustainable Travel Practices

1. Public Transportation and Carpooling:

Aspen offers an efficient and eco-friendly public transportation system operated by the Roaring Fork Transportation Authority (RFTA). Consider using buses to explore the town and nearby attractions. This not only reduces your carbon footprint but also helps alleviate traffic congestion. Additionally, carpooling with fellow travelers is a great way to minimize individual vehicle emissions.

2. Biking and Walking:

Explore Aspen's charming streets and scenic trails on a bicycle, which can be easily rented from various providers in town. Biking not only promotes a healthy lifestyle but also reduces air pollution. Choose walking as a mode of exploration, especially within the town center, to fully appreciate its unique atmosphere while minimizing environmental impact.

3. Waste Reduction:

Aspen is committed to waste reduction and recycling. Take advantage of designated recycling centers to dispose of your waste responsibly. Remember the mantra of "reduce, reuse, and recycle" to minimize the environmental impact of your visit. Make conscious choices, such as using reusable water bottles and bags, to decrease single-use plastic consumption.

4. Supporting Local and Sustainable Businesses:

Visit Aspen's vibrant farmers' markets to support local farmers and artisans. Purchase fresh, locally sourced produce and handmade crafts to contribute to the region's sustainability. Choosing local and sustainable businesses for dining and shopping helps stimulate the local economy and promotes responsible tourism.

5. Responsible Outdoor Recreation:

Adopt the principles of Leave No Trace when engaging in outdoor activities. Stay on designated trails to protect fragile ecosystems, respect wildlife by observing from a distance, and ensure that you pack out all waste. By following these principles, you play a crucial role in preserving the natural beauty of Aspen's outdoor spaces.

6. Energy Conservation:

Be mindful of energy consumption during your stay. Turn off lights, heating, and air conditioning when not in use. Choose accommodations that prioritize energy efficiency and sustainable practices. By being conscious of your energy usage, you contribute to Aspen's ongoing efforts to reduce its ecological footprint.

7. Cultural and Environmental Awareness:

Educate yourself about Aspen's cultural and environmental heritage. Understanding the significance of the region's ecosystems and local communities enhances your travel experience. Participate in guided eco-tours or cultural events to gain insights into Aspen's commitment to sustainability.

8. Water Conservation:

Aspen, like many mountainous regions, values water conservation. Conserve water by taking shorter showers and reusing towels during your hotel stay. Support restaurants and establishments that implement water-saving practices. Being mindful of water usage contributes to the sustainable management of this precious resource.

11.4 Health Precautions

Here are essential health precautions to keep in mind for a safe and enjoyable visit to Aspen.

1. Altitude Considerations:

- Hydration is Key: Aspen's elevation is around 8,000 feet (2,438 meters) above sea level. The high altitude can lead to dehydration, so it's crucial to drink plenty of water. Carry a reusable water bottle and sip water throughout the day to stay well-hydrated.

- Moderation with Alcohol: At higher altitudes, the effects of alcohol can be more pronounced. If you choose to indulge in alcoholic beverages, do so in moderation to avoid dehydration and altitude-related discomfort.

2. Sun Protection:

- Use Sunscreen Liberally: The sun's rays are more intense at higher elevations. Apply sunscreen with a high SPF to exposed skin, and reapply it regularly, especially if you're engaging in outdoor activities. Protecting your skin from sunburn is essential.
- Wear Sunglasses: Bring a pair of sunglasses with UV protection to shield your eyes from the intense mountain sunlight. This is particularly important when participating in snow-related activities, as the reflection from the snow can be intense.

3. Outdoor Safety:

- Weather Preparedness: Aspen's weather can be unpredictable, with sudden changes. Dress in layers, so you can adjust to temperature variations. Always check the weather forecast before heading outdoors, and carry essentials like rain gear and additional clothing.
- Know Your Limits: Whether you're hiking, skiing, or participating in any outdoor adventure, be aware of

your physical limits. Altitude can affect your stamina, so take breaks as needed and listen to your body.

4. Health Services:

- Pharmacies: Familiarize yourself with the locations of local pharmacies. Aspen has well-equipped pharmacies where you can purchase over-the-counter medications and health supplies if needed.
- Medical Facilities: Be aware of the nearest medical facilities and clinics. In case of any health concerns, seek prompt medical attention. Aspen Valley Hospital is the primary medical facility in the area.

5. COVID-19 Precautions:

- Stay Informed: Stay updated on local guidelines and any specific COVID-19 restrictions that may be in place. Regulations can change, so regularly check for the latest information from reliable sources.
- Follow Safety Measures: Adhere to recommended safety measures, including mask-wearing and social distancing, to protect yourself and others. Respect any specific guidelines established by businesses and public spaces.

CONCLUSION

Appendix: Additional Resources

As you wrap up your exploration of Aspen, it's essential to equip yourself with additional resources to enhance your understanding and appreciation of this captivating destination. The following resources provide valuable insights, practical information, and avenues for further exploration:

1. Aspen Chamber Resort Association (ACRA):

Website: Aspen Chamber Resort Association

Description: ACRA's official website is a comprehensive hub for tourist information, offering details on events, dining, accommodations, and local attractions. Stay updated on happenings and access valuable guides to plan future visits.

2. Aspen Times:

Website: Aspen Times

Description: The Aspen Times is a reliable source for local news, events, and insights into the community. Delve into articles and features that provide a deeper understanding of Aspen's dynamic culture and current affairs.

3. Aspen Trailheads:

Website: Aspen Trailheads

Description: For avid hikers and outdoor enthusiasts, AllTrails' Aspen section offers a plethora of trail information, including difficulty levels, user reviews, and detailed maps. Plan your next adventure with confidence.

4. Aspen Historical Society:

Website: Aspen Historical Society

Description: Dive into Aspen's rich history through the Aspen Historical Society. Explore exhibits, archives, and guided tours that illuminate the past, providing context to the town's evolution.

5. Aspen Snowmass:

Website: Aspen Snowmass

Description: Stay abreast of the latest developments in Aspen's winter sports scene through Aspen Snowmass. Access trail maps, weather updates, and event details to plan your visit during the snowy season.

These resources serve as invaluable companions, offering a deeper understanding of Aspen's past, present, and future. Whether you're planning a return trip or simply wish to stay connected with this enchanting destination, these avenues will keep the spirit of Aspen alive in your heart.

Additional Resources:

- Aspen Chamber of Commerce and Visitor Center: AspenChamber.org
- Trail Maps and Outdoor Guides: Aspen Trail Finder
- Cultural Event Calendars: Aspen Times Events
- Transportation Services: Roaring Fork Transportation Authority (RFTA)

- Weather and Seasonal Updates: AspenWeather.net
- Aspen's Official Website and Mobile Apps: City of Aspen

Final Thoughts and Recommendations

As your Aspen adventure draws to a close, it's natural to feel a mix of emotions – gratitude for the experiences, a sense of awe at nature's beauty, and perhaps a twinge of nostalgia. Aspen has a unique way of imprinting itself on the hearts of those who traverse its landscapes, leaving an enduring allure that beckons one back.

If time allows, consider taking a moment to savor Aspen's ambiance at a leisurely pace. Wander through the quaint streets, engage in conversations with locals, and relish the small yet significant details that define this mountain town. It's these subtle moments that often become the most cherished souvenirs of a journey.

As you reflect on your time in Aspen, think about the activities that resonated most with you. Was it the thrill of conquering the slopes, the serenity of a mountain hike, or the cultural immersion in Aspen's artistic and historic gems? Use these reflections to shape future travels and cultivate a deeper connection with destinations that align with your passions.

In recommending Aspen to fellow travelers, emphasize the diversity of experiences it offers. Whether seeking adventure on the mountains, cultural enrichment, or moments of quiet introspection, Aspen caters to a spectrum of interests. Encourage others to explore beyond the well-trodden paths, discovering hidden gems that add layers to the Aspen narrative.

Ultimately, Aspen's allure extends beyond its natural beauty; it's a destination that invites exploration, encourages introspection, and fosters a sense of connection with both the environment and the community. As you bid farewell to Aspen, carry these sentiments with you, knowing that the memories forged here will linger as a source of inspiration for future journeys.

Made in the USA
Middletown, DE
11 August 2024